Exploring the Bible
THE DICKINSON SERIES

WHAT IS THE BIBLE?

STUDENT TEXT

REV. ANNE ROBERTSON

FOREWORD BY DICKINSON SERIES BENEFACTOR,
DR. CHARLES C. DICKINSON, III

MASSACHUSETTS BIBLE SOCIETY
One Book, Many Voices

Massachusetts Bible Society
199 Herrick Road,
Newton Center, MA 02459

Book design by Thomas Bergeron
www.thomasbergeron.com
Typeface: Jenson Pro, Gill Sans

isbn-13: 978-0-615-64535-3

Photography Credits
Image #1 (p. xi) Foreword, Dr. Charles Dickinson, Courtesy of Dr. Charles Dickinson;
Image #3 (p. 20) Session 2, Old, torn Bible, Courtesy of Lydia Helene Irving (Flickr);
Image #11 (p. 75) Session 6, Temple Mount Wall, Courtesy of Joshua Paquin; Image
#13 (p. 79) Session 6, Translator/Dead Sea Scrolls, "Donald W. Parry, BYU, Study-
ing the Great Isaiah Scroll," Courtesy of Professor Donald W. Parry, BYU; Image #17
(p. 83) Session 6, Jesus Boat, Courtesy of Steven Kurtz; All other photos are public domain.

To Dr. Charles C. Dickinson
who, through his generosity, has given the Massachusetts Bible Society the opportunity to expand the knowledge of the Bible in ways that would not have been possible without his support.

TABLE OF **CONTENTS**

Aknowledgments

So many people have played a role in bringing this first course of *The Dickinson Series: Exploring the Bible* to life. Of course there is Dr. Dickinson, himself, to whom I have dedicated this first course; but there are also many others.

First there are the Trustees of the Massachusetts Bible Society who were willing to take a chance on this vision and allow me the time to develop the materials. From their editorial input, to their moral support, to their willingness to pilot classes in their communities, their engagement has been critical to making this a successful program.

Special thanks are also due to the parishes and leaders that piloted the course in their communities: First Parish Church in Weston, Massachusetts; First Unitarian Society in Newton, Massachusetts; Lutheran Church of the Newtons in Newton Center, Massachusetts; Sacred Heart Parish in Middleboro, Massachusetts; and St. Matthew's United Methodist Church in Acton, Massachusetts. Their feedback and willingness to work with unfinished materials allowed us to be absolutely certain that our finished product was worthy of your time and resources.

Of course the staff of the Massachusetts Bible Society: Jocelyn Bourgault, Mike Colyott, and Frank Stevens provided the backbone for the work. They handled logistics for facilitator training and pilot courses, hunted for illustrations, and picked up the many tasks that were flying off of my plate as I concentrated on this. They kept me on track and on budget and kept me sane. There is not a more awesome staff anywhere.

Finally, I am extremely grateful to editor Nancy Fitzgerald, copyeditor Jennifer Hackett, and designer Thomas Bergeron who took a rough diamond and made it shine. They have made my life so much easier and have provided creative and helpful input all along the way.

IN GRATITUDE,

Anne Robertson

WELCOME

The Bible. Just hearing the word makes some people sing and other people cringe. For some it conjures up images of crusades and inquisitions and preachers shaking their fists at unrepentant sinners. For others it evokes feelings of comfort, joy, and warm memories of Sunday School songs and church pageants. Still others respond with an eye to the culture, recognizing the hole that would be left in art, architecture, music, and literature without the rich base of stories and imagery in the pages of the Bible.

So what's the deal? How does the person who would like to find out more about the Bible navigate that sea of conflicting ideas, emotions, and interpretations? How do you even stick your toe in those waters without drowning or being led so far from shore that you can't find your way back?

Well, it just so happens that we have this set of courses...

INTRODUCING THE DICKINSON SERIES: EXPLORING THE BIBLE

The Dickinson Series: Exploring the Bible is a series of four, six-week courses with a concluding conference that leads to a Certificate in Biblical Literacy from the historic Massachusetts Bible Society.

Each of the four courses is designed to fit six, ninety-minute sessions with a group of eight to fifteen people. The Massachusetts Bible Society provides training, materials, and ongoing support for those who would like to run the program in their local churches or communities. Those leading the courses are not expected to be biblical experts or pastors. They are those gifted and trained to facilitate a warm, welcoming, and open group environment where the material can be presented and discussed with respect for all participants.

The concluding conference is designed by the Massachusetts Bible Society and hosted at a single location.

The Dickinson Series Program

FOUR COURSES: A BIRD'S-EYE VIEW

I. **What is The Bible?** A broad overview of the Bible, including chapters on how to select a Bible suitable for your needs, how the Bible is organized, how the collection of books that comprise the Bible were chosen, different ways that people approach the text, and what archaeology has to tell us about the text and its stories.

II. **Introducing the Old Testament.** A look at the best-known stories, most influential passages, and unforgettable characters that comprise the Old Testament. What are the primary themes and narratives? What are the characteristics of ancient Hebrew literature and the mindset of people in the ancient Near East?

III. **Introducing the New Testament.** Similar in scope to *Introducing the Old Testament*, with some attention to other works—including gospels, letters, and other writings—that were not included in the New Testament but that were important in the early church.

IV. **The Bible in Context.** A look at the culture and historical events surrounding the various times of the biblical narrative. Looking into biblical professions, economies, and politics as well as the ways that events, invasions, science, and culture in other parts of the world have had an impact on the biblical texts.

THE DICKINSON SERIES CONFERENCE

Each spring, the Massachusetts Bible Society hosts the Dickinson Series Conference at a location in Massachusetts. This multi-day event includes lectures by scholars and teachers and workshops by religious leaders who bring expertise in specific biblical topics to complement the basics learned in the four courses. At the conclusion of the conference, certificates are awarded to those who have completed the series and enrollment opens for the next year. The conference also provides time for social interaction and entertainment.

ONLINE RESOURCES

The initial courses have an online component. In addition to exercises that entail doing some research on the Internet, there are forums on the massbible. org website where those participating in courses in any location can come together, share stories, ask questions, and discuss perspectives.

COMPLETION TIME FRAME

The courses are designed so that a certificate can be obtained within one year. This would entail finding groups for two courses in the fall and two in the spring, and then attending the conference.

We recognize, however, that such a compressed time frame may not be possible for all students. With that in mind, the initial enrollment fee is good for five years. If the program has not been completed in that time, enrollment may be extended for up to two years for a small additional fee. All fees are forfeited if the certificate is not obtained within seven years and must be paid in full again if a student wants to continue.

Although enrollment fees would need to be paid again to continue past seven years, any course fully completed may be carried beyond the seven years as long as the materials used for the completed course(s) are still current. If the materials used have been revised, the course will have to be completed with the new materials before credit can be issued.

The Dickinson Series Students

The series is designed for two distinct types of students:

The Intentional or "Extra Mile" Students. This first group represents those who have determined that they really want to do some work to build a strong foundation for Bible study. They might be Christians considering seminary, people of faith who don't know their own Scriptures very well, people of other faiths who want a clearer understanding of the Christian text, or even people of no faith who recognize the cultural and geo political influence of the Bible and want to understand it better. The common denominator among this first group is that they want to do the whole program, including the "Extra Mile" assignments required to earn the certificate or Continuing Education Units (CEUs).

The Casual or Informal Students. The second group is made up of those who might know something about the Bible but have gaps in their knowledge or those who just want to test the waters of biblical studies. These students might want simply to take one of the four courses, attend the conference, or put together some combination of those components without doing all that is necessary to complete the certificate program. While it's expected that this second group will still actively participate in whatever course(s) they select, there is less work expected of them outside the group setting.

We hope each study group will consist of both casual and more intentional learners, and our design includes opportunities in class sessions for those engaging the material more deeply to share what they've learned with the others.

The Dickinson Series Sponsors

THE BENEFACTOR

The Dickinson Series is named in honor of its chief benefactor, Dr. Charles C. Dickinson III, a biblical scholar and long-time trustee of the Massachusetts Bible Society. Dr. Charles Dickinson was born in Charleston, West Virginia, on May 13, 1936; was educated there and at Phillips Academy, Andover, Massachusetts; and graduated cum laude in religion and philosophy from Dartmouth College, Hanover, New Hampshire. After serving three and a half years with the US Marine Corps in the USA and Far East, he studied theology and philosophy in Chicago, Pittsburgh, West and East Germany, at Yale University and Union Theological Seminary (New York); received his B.D. (Bachelor of Divinity) and Ph.D. degrees in Pittsburgh in 1965 and 1973 respectively; and did post-doctoral study at Oxford University and Harvard Divinity School. Dr. Dickinson has taught in Richmond Virginia; Kinshasa, Zaïre, Congo; Charleston, West Virginia; Rome, Italy; the People's Republic of China; Andover Newton Theological School; and Beacon Hill Seminars in Boston. He lives with his wife, JoAnne, and their son, John, in Boston.

THE AUTHOR

This series was conceived and designed by Rev. Anne Robertson, executive director of the Massachusetts Bible Society, who also developed and wrote the four student texts and leader's guides. She is the author of three books: *Blowing the Lid Off the God-Box: Opening Up to a Limitless Faith* (Morehouse, 2005); *God's Top 10: Blowing the Lid Off the Commandments* (Morehouse, 2006); and *God With Skin On: Finding God's Love in Human Relationships* (Morehouse, 2009). Rev. Robertson is an elder in the New England Conference of the United Methodist Church, is a winner of the Wilbur C. Ziegler

Award for Excellence in Preaching, and is a sought-after speaker and workshop leader. She can be found on the web at www.annerobertson.org.

Founded on July 6, 1809, the Massachusetts Bible Society is an ecumenical, Christian organization that has historically been a place where those across the theological spectrum of belief could unite for a common purpose. At the beginning of its history, that purpose was simply getting a copy of the Bible into the hands of anyone who wanted one, especially those without the means or opportunity to obtain one themselves.

In more recent times, that work has been supplemented by the development of a variety of educational programs highlighting the importance of the Bible for faith, culture, history, and politics as well as providing a forum for the many different voices of biblical interpretation. This Series is a significant addition to those efforts and attempts to continue the historic tradition of being a place where those across the theological spectrum can unite for a common purpose—in this case, biblical literacy. You can find out more about the Massachusetts Bible Society at www.massbible.org.

YOU

The Dickinson Series is made possible because you have elected to be a part of it. While we believe the course materials are useful in and of themselves, it is the community of students and facilitators that bring those materials to life as you engage with one another in your classes and in the online forums. Just by participating you are helping to raise the level of biblical literacy in our world.

You can ensure that this ministry continues by sending in the facilitator and student evaluations for each course, by purchasing the materials, and by telling others about the Dickinson Series. There are also opportunities for you to provide scholarship assistance for future students, to attend training to become a facilitator, or simply to offer moral or financial support to the mission of the Massachusetts Bible Society. Our biggest sponsor is you.

OUR THEOLOGICAL POINT OF VIEW

In the creation of this series there are several obvious biases:

- The Bible is a book that can and should be read by individuals both inside and outside the church.

- Understanding of the Bible is enhanced and deepened in conversation with others.

- The tools of scholarship are not incompatible with a faithful reading of Scripture.

- Diversity of opinion is both a welcome and a necessary part of any education.

Beyond those points we have tried to give an unbiased theological perspective, describing differences of opinion and scholarship in neutral terms.

Although named for and written by Christians, the Dickinson Series is designed to be an educational tool, not an evangelistic tool. The Massachusetts Bible Society affirms that the making of Christian disciples is the job of the local church. These materials are designed either to fit into the overall disciple-making effort of a local church or into a secular environment where people of other faiths or of no faith can gain a deeper understanding of the nature and content of the Bible.

COURSE ADMINISTRATION

Obtaining Credit for Certification or CEUs

Those wishing to enroll in the certificate program or obtain CEUs for their work must fill out an application and do the work in an approved small-group setting. Those who simply work their way through the materials on their own are not eligible for credit or certification.

Each course in the series will involve nine hours of class time and about fifteen hours of preparation outside of class. Upon successful completion of each course, you may earn two and a half CEUs. To find out more or to obtain an application, go to www.massbible.org/dickinson-series-application.

The Cost

Costs will vary depending on whether you are a casual student or taking the course either for CEUs or certification. Please check our website at www.massbible.org/dickinson-series for more information, current rates, and information on discounts and scholarships.

Keeping in Touch

Go to www.massbible.org/dickinson-series to learn more or contact the Massachusetts Bible Society at 199 Herrick Road, Newton Center, MA 02459 or admin@massbible.org. You may also call us at 617-969-9404.

FOREWORD

Dr. Charles Dickinson

It is my great honor and pleasure to introduce *The Dickinson Series: Exploring the Bible*, not only to regular or occasional Bible readers, but also to those who have never opened a Bible, yet are curious about what might be contained between its mysterious covers. After all, along with Shakespeare, the Bible has influenced Western culture—including American culture—more strongly than any other single book. More importantly, it has had an unparalleled influence on what we think is right and wrong, good and bad, worthy and unworthy—an influence we might be totally unaware of until we study other cultures and find that they may have values very different from our own. Finally, the Bible offers us not only a moral guide for life, but a reason and strength for living a *good* life. It is a source unequalled by any other philosophy or religion on the face of the earth.

But in Bible study as with other endeavors there is no free lunch. Let me use biblical metaphors: Even if you find a treasure buried in a field, you still have to buy the field and dig up the treasure. Even if you find a pearl of great price at a steep discount, you still need enough money to buy the pearl (Matthew 13:44–45). And so it is with the Bible: If you really want to understand it and profit from it, you can't just skim it and toss it aside, like a cheap paperback novel. You have to study it and become familiar with it.

But that's not as hard as you might think, for the Bible consists largely of *stories*, stories that don't just tell you what to do, but how God—the ultimate source of all value, moral and otherwise—has acted in history and still acts in it today to make our lives truly human in the very best sense. The Bible also contains laws that embodied what constituted a good life for the ancient Hebrews, though some may no longer work for our day and age. It contains songs and poems, some called "Psalms," prayers from the depth of the psalmist's suffering or sung as hymns in praise of God; and others, as in the "Song of Songs," that are beautiful love poems. And the Bible even contains detailed instructions on how to live a good life, both individually and in community: how to treat your loved ones, and your neighbors near and far, well instead of badly.

Let me illustrate my point about the value of coming to grips with the Bible by contrasting two different approaches to it. The first I might call the "fundamentalist evangelical" approach to the Bible. Many take that approach because, as they say, Jesus Christ has changed their lives. That I believe, and heartily affirm, and can even say the same for myself. In fact, I think that for those of us who attest to such a changed life, Jesus Christ has effected a "salvation," not just in the next world but in our present lives here on earth. But those who take what I have called the "fundamentalist evangelical" approach to the Bible have, by definition, accepted the whole fundamentalist package— that, if you are going to be a Christian, then you must take every single word of the Bible literally. Now I myself was raised in a Southern Presbyterian, implicitly fundamentalist context. Though we weren't told that we must believe *every single word* of the Bible literally, we did learn that the Bible was the word of God and that we had no reason to question it.

But then I went off in a different and, to my mind, better direction, along what I might call the "high road" of serious biblical scholarship. Since my teens I have learned to take a more critical look at the Bible, to use all the tools of critical scholarship when studying it, and to accept much of the critical scholarship on it by Protestants, Catholics, and Jews. Thus, leaving fundamentalism behind me, I have brought the Bible all the closer to me by digging deep into it, and trying to find out what it has to say to me—and to us—in all its many layers of narrative, of history, of song, and of theology. The great Protestant theologian Reinhold Niebuhr reminded us in his *Interpretation of Christian Ethics* to take the Bible less literally, yet more seriously.

Like many of Reinhold Niebuhr's friends and colleagues, I would call myself a "liberal evangelical": "Evangelical" because I continue to believe and confess that Jesus Christ has saved me, not just in the next world but in my life here on earth. "Evangelical" means one who believes and preaches the good news of Christ, and that is what I do. But I also consider myself "liberal," because the gospel itself leads me to open myself to many modern currents of thought—including both modern critical biblical scholarship and modern science—to engage their findings and to accept many of them, testing all things, as the Apostle Paul says, and keeping what is good. (1 Thessalonians 5:21) Being liberal in this sense involves a lot of ongoing theological and biblical reworking and rethinking—the word liberal means liberty-loving, and that invokes the "freedom" for which "Christ has set us free" and to which we have been "called." (Galatians 5:1, 13)

For me—and I hope for you, too—engaging in biblical scholarship is an enormous help in my own reading of the Bible. It opens up for me so many biblical passages that otherwise I would find hard to understand. Though the Bible is inspired by God, it is inspired by a God who has entrusted the actual *writing* of it to human beings just like us; thus it is also a very *human* collection of documents from a time-span of over a thousand years. I can only rejoice at attempting—by means of the Dickinson Series—to open up to a wide audience of believers and others the fascinating literary, historical, and theological investigations into this "treasure in earthen vessels"—the Bible.

—Charles Dickinson
Boston, Massachusetts
February 20, 2012

TO THE STUDENT

Welcome to the first of four courses in *The Dickinson Series: Exploring the Bible*. Most people who decide to study the Bible attempt to do so by just diving in. They get a Bible and start reading on page 1, often expecting that it will flow in some kind of orderly succession to the end.

While it's not impossible to study the Bible that way, it may not be the most helpful strategy, because the Bible is a different sort of book. In fact, it isn't even really accurate to call the Bible a "book;" it's more like an anthology of texts, collected in one bound volume, that have become sacred to a variety of religious traditions. Without some understanding of what the Bible is and isn't, conflicts about its contents can easily escalate.

Most of the arguments and conflicts over the Bible aren't really about what the Bible says, but about how to interpret what it says. At their root, the conflicts represent different ways that people approach the book as a whole as well as differences in what sort of book they believe the Bible to be. We'll examine a number of those differences during this course.

For example, the debates about creationism versus evolution aren't about what the Bible says per se. They're about whether what the Bible says should be read as religious truth (and therefore full of metaphor and symbol), as scientific fact (and therefore if the text says "seven days," it means precisely seven twenty-four-hour periods), or as a historical document that describes what an ancient people once believed about the creation of the world.

This first course will allow you to dip your toes into some of the more famous stories and passages of the Bible as you read and discuss parts of the text itself. The broader purpose, however, is to take you up to the balcony that overlooks several thousand years of history and to help you to understand how we got this particular collection of ancient texts into a bound volume called the Bible.

QUESTIONS, PLEASE!

You'll probably finish this first course with more questions than you had at the beginning—or at least with a different set of questions. So it's important to see yourself less as a typical student in a classroom and more as an explorer or investigative reporter. Learning to ask good, incisive questions is more important to the learning process than memorizing answers that have been handed to you.

Don't be afraid of your questions and try not to be frustrated if there doesn't appear to be an easy answer. When dealing in the realm of religion (whether that religion represents your faith or not) people often spend entire lifetimes seeking answers and sometimes the only "answer" available will be a variety of opinions. Even on matters that seem like they should have verifiable, factual answers, like "Who wrote this text?" or "When did this happen?" the response, "No one really knows but there are several schools of thought" is more common than you might expect.

As questions arise for you, write them down. Especially if you plan to go on to other courses in the Dickinson Series or even other Bible studies in other places, keeping a journal of your questions and thoughts can be very helpful. You may find that some of your early issues are settled later on. At the very least, be sure your question is raised either in your group or in the online forums. If you have the question, you can bet someone else does also, and if it turns out that a lot of people are asking the very same question, we can revise this text to address it for others down the road.

From the second session onward, there will be an opportunity for each person to ask a question about the material at the very beginning of each class, and there is a section at the end of each session in this text to encourage you to think about your questions ahead of that "check-in" time. These "check-in" questions will be recorded by your facilitator but not immediately addressed, as many of them may be dealt with during the ensuing class(es).

You'll also be learning about the various Bible study tools and resources available to you, so that you can seek out your own answers. See Appendix 4 (p. 96) for a list of tools and resources to help you find answers to your questions.

DIVERSITY HELPS YOU LEARN

The Dickinson Series isn't designed solely for people of Christian faith. It is our hope that people of other faiths, or even of no faith, who wish to better understand the Christian Scriptures can engage with this series to learn more about the book that has shaped so much of the world's culture, politics, and even geography. We hope that many groups will have a mix of people learning about the Bible for a variety of reasons and coming from different perspectives.

We learn very little when we're only exposed to thinking that mirrors our own, and we encourage every person using this book for study to find a way to engage others in dialogue. Ideally that's your small group of eight to fifteen people who get to know one another over the six-week period. But if you're doing the study on your own, try to visit the forums on the massbible.org website to see what others who are studying the same text are asking and talking about. This will enhance your learning experience.

PICK YOUR LEVEL OF ENGAGEMENT

The Dickinson Series has two different levels of engagement and you may well have both represented in your group. In fact, class sessions have been designed with the assumption that most groups will have both kinds of students in the same group.

As explained in the Introduction, the series of four courses is designed to culminate in a Certificate of Biblical Literacy and each of the four courses can be taken for Continuing Education Units (CEUs), which might be required for various professional organizations. Students seeking either certification or CEUs are asked to do extra work to earn that recognition. We have called this group the Extra Mile students and at the end of each session in the student text, you'll see an additional homework assignment just for them.

We expect, however, that other students will simply engage the course from a sense of general interest. Some may feel that only one or two of the four courses would be helpful to them or that their current circumstances would not allow for doing the extra work. These "informal" students also have homework, but to a much lesser degree.

Of course, any "informal" student is welcome to do the Extra Mile exercises simply to delve deeper into a topic of interest. Several class sessions have time set aside for those who have done the Extra Mile work (no matter to which category of student they belong) to share what they've learned with others in the group.

Whichever group you're in, check out the homework for each session before you decide to leave it until the last minute. Extra Mile students can always count on a couple of hours per session for their homework, but the informal student homework ramps up from about twenty to thirty minutes for the first couple of sessions to about an hour and a half later on. Plan ahead.

As with most everything in life, you'll get out of this course what you put into it or, as the Bible so aptly puts it, "You reap whatever you sow." (Galatians 6:7) If you're an "Extra Mile" student, not doing the work will waste your money and cost you your certificate or CEUs. If you're an "informal" student, you simply won't learn as much and the others in the group will be deprived of the insights, questions, and opinions that you might have otherwise contributed. You came here to learn, so don't shortchange yourself. Do the work.

FOR THE CHRISTIAN STUDENT

If you're coming to this class as a Christian seeking to enrich your faith by engaging your own sacred text, you'll almost certainly have different kinds of questions than those who want to learn about the Bible for other reasons. Information in this course and others may challenge some of your basic faith assumptions. Be assured that there are literally millions of Christians with a deep, Spirit-filled, Christ-centered faith who have found their faith grounded and strengthened by some of the very questions that once felt strange or threatening to them.

Hang with it. Keep a journal to record your feelings and your questions. Bring them to your specific faith community, raise them on the forums, talk with members of your group who share your faith. Pray about the issues that arise for you. Christian faith is never static. It is a journey during which we change and grow along the way. Sometimes we take a wrong path and have to cut through the brambles to get back on track, and other times we come out of a hard climb to suddenly see the most splendid view.

The questions you have will be your own and you will be the one sorting through the variety of responses to see what resonates in your spirit. The Bible itself is full of people having their faith challenged by the circumstances they face or the information they obtain, and none of them are struck by lightning for their honest searching. If you find yourself in such a place, remember the words from Joshua 1:9: "Be strong and courageous. Do not be afraid; do not be discouraged, for the LORD your God will be with you wherever you go."

Be sure to recognize, however, that the goal of this course is to make the Bible more understandable and accessible to all people, regardless of their faith perspective. If you have people of other faiths or of no faith in your group, recognize and respect those differences in your questions and discussions. Trust the Bible to speak in its own way to those who choose to study it for their own reasons.

FOR STUDENTS OUTSIDE THE CHRISTIAN TRADITION

While the Bible contains texts that are sacred to both the Jewish and Muslim faiths, the Dickinson Series is examining the text as it is used in Christian communities. It is more than likely that there will be some in your group taking this class for reasons related to their Christian faith and their questions and comments will often be quite different from yours.

It is difficult to truly understand the Bible apart from hearing the perspectives of those who turn to this set of texts as part of their faith. At the Massachusetts Bible Society, we recognize that the use of the Bible by Christians has at times been harmful, oppressive, and counter to the very faith Christians claim to represent. We also believe, however, that such uses are not the inevitable result of a Bible-based faith.

We have tried in this book and in the class exercises to present the sacred text of Christians in a way that is welcoming of those who want to know more about it for other reasons. Our goal in the Dickinson Series is educational rather than evangelical. This doesn't mean you won't hear a variety of Christian perspectives and/or debates, but it does mean that you should not feel pressured to adopt the Christian faith or engage those debates on any basis other than their own merits.

GIVE US FEEDBACK!

If the Bible is taught in public schools it excludes the faith perspective. If it is taught in a religious setting it often either ignores or attempts to discredit secular issues and perspectives. The Dickinson Series seeks to include both perspectives and all kinds of students in mixed groups and with the same study—and that is perhaps our greatest challenge with this material. We welcome your feedback regarding the success of our efforts and you'll find an evaluation at the end of this text.

R-E-S-P-E-C-T

You are about to engage with others in reading, talking, and learning about the Bible. For some, the Bible is the text that led them to encounter God and can have deep and powerful resonance. For some, what seems like a simple question about the Bible can be heard as an attack on everything they know to be true and believe.

Others may have experienced the Bible as an instrument of great harm in their personal relationships or learned about its negative effects in history and politics. For still others, the Bible is a curiosity—a foreign object about which they have no strong feelings.

The conflicts between faith traditions and the conflicts in our culture can easily become evident in your group. You have the chance in this study to model something our culture desperately needs—civil and respectful dialogue about important and meaningful differences.

Don't be a hater. Don't flame the forums. Don't rant in your group or condemn the perspectives of others. If you find a discussion is raising strong feelings and you don't know how to express them with respect, you can always say, "I'm having a very strong reaction to this and don't know how to express it well." Your facilitator (or a moderator on the forums) can then help move the group forward.

DEFINING THE ERA: NOTATING THE DATE

When it comes to measuring time, Western culture has often adopted the calendar of Christianity, which puts the birth of Jesus at the center of history. In the Christian calendar everything that happened before that time is notated as B.C. (before Christ) and everything afterwards as A.D. (*Anno Domini* in Latin, meaning "the year of the Lord"). According to Merriam-Webster, the first known use of A.D. in a system of dating was in 1512.

It is no surprise that other faiths and other cultures have retained their own methods of dating the years, which then becomes problematic in a global culture trying to figure out a common way to measure time. This problem has been addressed by an academic compromise of keeping the year zero as it has been on the Christian calendar, but adopting a more neutral system of describing the years before and after. In that compromise system what Christians refer to as Before Christ (B.C.) becomes Before the Christian (or Common) Era (B.C.E.) and what Christians refer to as Anno Domini (A.D.) becomes simply the Christian (or Common) Era (C.E.).

Because we want this course to be a resource for all who want to know about the Bible—regardless of their religious beliefs—we have adopted the more neutral B.C.E. and C.E. system of annotating time.

ORIENTATION
TO THE BIBLE

Any Bible*

This Student Text

Pen and paper or laptop for taking notes

*Session 2 will guide you in selecting a study Bible for use in later lessons.
For Session 1 any Bible will do. Your group facilitator will have a Bible for you
to use if you don't have one to bring.

VANESSA'S STORY

The billboard was huge and Vanessa had no trouble reading it in the slow high-way traffic. "Judgment Day is coming on May 21. The Bible is never wrong. Be prepared." Vanessa chuckled to herself. "Couldn't the world end now?" she wondered. "This traffic is making me crazy."

But still she thought about it. Vanessa didn't really know much about the Bible. Her family had not been churchgoers, although they always had called themselves Christians. But Sundays were typically filled with other things and before she knew it, Vanessa was grown and married and continuing life in much the same way. Jesus seemed like a decent guy, and she taught her kids to share, to be polite, and to avoid the "bad crowd." Wasn't that the essence of it? Honestly, she didn't know.

The Bible had been in her face a lot this week, especially from her son. Jeremy had begun to show a real interest in art and just yesterday she had taken him to the city museum.

"Mom, what's happening in that painting?" he had asked, time and time again.

Her answer was always the same. "It's a Bible story, honey."

"But what's happening?" Jeremy persisted.

Vanessa was embarrassed that she had no more information to give him. She wasn't even really sure they *were* Bible stories, but that's what she said when she saw someone in the painting with a halo.

And then there had been the letter from her representative in Congress. It asked for her support and claimed that the government had strayed far from the principles of the Bible and the faith of our founding fathers. Well, she couldn't say for sure whether that was true or not. Was she being asked to vote for a godly man or a religious fanatic? She had no way of knowing.

Before she knew what she was doing, Vanessa had left the traffic jam behind and taken the exit for the mall. "I need to just get a Bible and read it," she thought. "This is silly. I think I'm well educated, but I don't know even basic answers to things that affect my son's education or my ability to vote wisely. And should I be preparing for that meeting on May 22? Could the world really be coming to an end?" Soon the large brick façade of the bookstore loomed.

When Vanessa finally found the section of Bibles, she discovered that it made the traffic jam seem preferable. There were tons of the things—all different. First were all sorts of different English translations, although some were called "paraphrases." What was that about? There were Bibles for those in recovery, for women, for children, for those interested in archaeology. There were "study" Bibles

and "devotional" Bibles. Some had highlights in red, some highlighted different things in green, and still others had different verses in purple. There was the Poverty and Justice Bible, the Amplified Bible, the New Spirit-Filled Life Bible. To top it all off, some Bibles included books that other Bibles didn't. Her eyes began to blur. She left empty-handed.

WHY ALL THE PROBLEMS?

To her dismay, Vanessa discovered what many people have discovered: You can't just "go get a Bible" with ease anymore. It used to be simple, even fifty years ago. But today, it can be as confusing to select a copy of the Bible as it is to find the "healthy" loaf of bread in the grocery store.

Why is reading the Bible different from reading other books, and why is it so daunting just to pick out a copy? There are a lot of reasons.

1. The Bible is not like other books.

- It contains sacred text for three of the world's major religions (Christianity, Judaism, and Islam).

- It's not really one book, but many, and even different Christian traditions include different books.

- Multiple authors wrote it across more than a millennium.

- It includes a large variety of types of literature—history, letters, prophecy, poetry, narrative, legal documents, building specifications, and more.

- It was originally written in languages that now are only the languages of academic disciplines.

- Lots of people feel very strongly about what the Bible "means." And they don't agree. Not even scholars.

All of that can be quite daunting and yet there are equally strong reasons to try to navigate the Bible's tricky waters. Cultural references to the Bible are everywhere and people quote it all the time for all kinds of reasons.

BIBLE REFERENCING

The earliest biblical scrolls don't separate passages into chapters and verses as contemporary Bibles do. Those aids were added in the Middle Ages.

The traditional way to reference a passage in the Bible is by citing first the book, and then the chapter number followed by a colon and the verse number(s). So, for example, the command to "love your neighbor as yourself" is found in the book of Leviticus, chapter 19, verse 18. It is notated as Leviticus 19:18.

2. The Bible is everywhere. Biblical allusions can be found throughout our language, literature, art, music, and architecture—it's difficult to claim a cultural education without at least a passing knowledge of the basic stories and texts of the Bible.

Rembrandt created over three hundred works of art on biblical themes. If your children enjoyed *The Chronicles of Narnia*, they enjoyed an allegorical interpretation of Christ's passion. Literary works by Tolstoy, Dickens, Flannery O'Connor, Dante, Milton, Steinbeck, Shakespeare, and a host of others are rife with biblical references. There are hospitals and charitable organizations across the country and around the globe that take their name from Jesus' parable of the Good Samaritan.

As a case in point, try out the following exercise to see how the Bible permeates the English language.

I Heard It in the Bible: Look up the following passages (your Bible should have a table of contents to help you find the books) and see if you can determine what common English phrase or idiom comes from that passage. Answers can be found at the end of this session.

Isaiah 40:15	Matthew 15:14
Matthew 5:13	Job 15:7
Genesis 3:3	Job 19:20
Revelation 16:16	I Timothy 6:12
Ecclesiastes 10:1	Matthew 5:41
Matthew 12:25	

NOTE: *For those using a pre-2010 edition of the New American Bible, the Ecclesiastes reference above is found in Ecclesiastes 9:18 instead of Ecclesiastes 10:1.*

3. The Bible plays a role in politics. Biblical claims, for good or for ill, also play a role in American political life, and many of the histories of nations described in the Bible are still being played out in the geopolitics of the world today. The complexities of Middle East conflicts are deeply interwoven with biblical texts. There's a whole lot that can't be understood about our world without at least some familiarity with the Bible, whether you see it as a sacred text or just another book. Its influence on history, culture, and contemporary society is too large to ignore. Of course those who do claim the

FOR **REFLECTION**

When have you encountered references to the Bible outside of a religious setting?

How did you respond?

Have you ever been in a situation in which you felt awkward not knowing what was in the Bible?

What has sparked your interest in knowing more?

Bible as the sacred text of their faith need to dig in for the sake of their own spiritual growth.

A July 2011 Gallup poll found that three in ten Americans believe that the Bible should be interpreted literally, and some political leader is being named as the Antichrist almost as frequently as someone is predicting the end of the world based on biblical prophecy. The Bible crops up wherever you go.

4. The Bible can be hard to understand. For a long time the complexities of the Bible and the difficulties of getting books into people's hands put the complete burden of conveying its contents on the church and clergy. Gutenberg's printing press, Bible translators, and changing sensibilities have altered all that. You can now get a Bible in your own language, access all sorts of study guides and information, and shape your own faith accordingly. In fact, there is now so much information available at the click of a mouse that it can be hard to know what sources to trust. That is one of many reasons to do serious Bible study in a community setting.

THE BIBLE AND THE FABRIC OF LIFE

Nobody reads the Bible in a vacuum. How we interpret what we read is influenced by our own life experiences, our current circumstances, and even the neurons in our brains. As Christians read the Bible, it is always good to pray for guidance from the Holy Spirit, but there are also other things that can make reading the Bible more fruitful for anyone.

THE ROLE OF COMMUNITY

One of the reasons the church was so wary of letting everyone have access to the biblical texts (those who first attempted to translate the Bible into English

FOR **REFLECTION**

What have been your experiences of learning in a group setting?

What made them good or bad?

Have you had any experience with religious community of any kind?

What were the pros and cons of those groups?

Do you have close friends or relatives who have strongly different views than yours (about religion or anything else important to you)?

Have you ever changed your mind from hearing the perspective of someone else?

were burned at the stake) is the fact that the Bible is so complex. It just takes one person with some charisma and a personality disorder to misuse the Bible for some horrible ends, recruiting others to the cause with disastrous results. David Koresh and the cult at Waco, Texas, in the early 1990s is a good example.

The best way to learn about the Bible is to learn within a community. Each of us reads the same words on the page, but we each read through the lens of our own lives and experiences. Hearing the different ways that others react to the same Bible stories and texts, and hearing how those texts have been traditionally interpreted gives us a much better foundation for making a decision than just our own reading.

The best Bible study is a combination of our own direct reading and understanding, learning what scholars and faith tradition have to say, and discussing both of those things with a diverse group of people who are doing the same thing. If all of those interpretations are in agreement, then your foundation is not broad enough. Seek out different interpretations so that your own understanding is on solid ground.

THE ROLE OF YOUR BRAIN

If you haven't figured it out by now, you will need your brain for this study. You don't need to be Einstein, but you can't just sit back and have someone tell you what it all means and what to think about it. Plenty of people do that, but it is a dangerous posture to take in a world of scams, cults, and hucksters. This is a study to open the world of the Bible to you and to help you find the questions and issues that each of us must sort out for ourselves.

The Biases of This Course

To the degree possible, we have tried to present the information without bias. However, this course does contain three foundational biases:

Universal access. The Bible can and should be both read and interpreted by any interested individuals in conversation with scholarship, faith tradition, and a community of others doing the same thing.

The importance of scholarship. There are those who believe scholarship has no place in the study of Scripture and that the Holy Spirit does all the interpretation necessary. There are also those who believe that the traditional interpretations by the church and faith communities are too filled with political and other hidden agendas to be trusted. Still others want to hear only the voices of agreement. This study believes that scholarship has a constructive role to play in conversation with a diversity of faith traditions and interpretations.

A smidge of skepticism. This series sees skepticism as an important and even necessary tool in real study. That said, it also endorses the concept that the checks and balances offered by the combination of our own reasoning ability, the voices of a diversity of others, the discoveries of scholarship, and the anchor of faith tradition allow us to build a solid foundation that is worthy of our trust.

> **FOR REFLECTION**
>
> We all tend to trust some sources and be skeptical of others. What sources do you automatically trust for information or guidance?
>
> What sources do you feel you need to double-check?
>
> Are there sources you simply will not believe no matter what?
>
> What do you trust the Bible to tell you?
>
> What don't you trust the Bible to tell you?

CHOOSING A BIBLE

You've probably already figured out that choosing a Bible is complicated. To make the selection that's right for you, try this: Read through "To the Student" on page xv and Session 1 beginning on page 1 if you have not already done so. Read through the material for Session 2 and, on the basis of that information, select the Bible you will use for this study. Get a *study* Bible in a particular *translation.* Look over the selections in a bookstore or online (there are e-versions of many study Bibles) and pick one. After reading through Session 2 and surveying the options, if you still cannot decide, here are some suggestions to help you make up your mind:

- If you have no church affiliation and lean liberal, go with a study Bible based on the New Revised Standard Version. If you lean conservative, the New International Version is your choice. Neither is on the radical end, so it doesn't make a huge difference. I have both on my shelf and have used both extensively. As of this writing, the New International Version is not available with the Apocrypha (See p. 19).

- If you're Protestant and attend church, check the translation of the Bibles in the pews and get a study Bible version of that translation. If there are no Bibles in the pews, ask your pastor for a recommendation.

- If you're Roman Catholic, you'll want the New American Bible, New Revised Standard Version, or Revised Standard Version. When selecting one of the latter, be sure to get one with the Apocrypha included. If you're active in a parish, ask your priest for a recommendation if you can't decide.

E-VERSIONS

The Bible is, of course, all over the Internet and you can get phone apps with more Bible translations than Disney has dalmatians. There are also many, many sites, apps, and other electronic media with a variety of Bible study tools. The advantage of an actual study Bible (either print or e-book) is that you have a variety of tools in one location that have been vetted by scholars. If you want to delve into any topic more, you can find some recommended study resources at massbible.org/how-to-study-bible.

- If you're Orthodox and don't read the original Greek, get the Orthodox Study Bible.

HOMEWORK

(ALL STUDENTS)

☐ Read through Session I material and study the sections on "The Bible and the Fabric of Life" (p. 5) and "Choosing a Bible" (p. 7).

☐ Read through Session 2 material in the Student Text and respond in writing to the two questions at the end of Session 2 on page 23 in preparation for class check-in.

☐ Select and obtain the study Bible you will use for the remainder of this course.

EXTRA MILE

(CEU AND CERTIFICATE STUDENTS)

☐ Read the section in Session I called "The Role of Your Brain" (p. 6-7).

☐ Using the reflection questions at the end of that section as a guide, write an essay of approximately five hundred words on the issues of trust and skepticism raised by the Bible. This is a reflective rather than an academic essay and you will not be asked to share it during Session 2. What are the issues for you?

(If purchasing a study Bible is beyond your means, please speak privately to your group leader or contact the Massachusetts Bible Society. Scholarship help is available.)

ANSWER KEY FOR "I HEARD IT IN THE BIBLE": *1. Drop in the bucket 2. Salt of the earth 3. Forbidden fruit 4. Armageddon 5. Fly in the ointment 6. A house divided against itself cannot stand 7. The blind leading the blind 8. As old as the hills 9. By the skin of your teeth 10. Fight the good fight. 11. Go the extra mile.*

CHOOSING
A BIBLE

MATERIALS YOU WILL NEED FOR YOUR SECOND CLASS SESSION:

The study Bible you have selected to use for this course

Responses to the Check-in questions on page 23

Extra Mile homework if applicable

This Student Text

Pen and paper or laptop for taking notes

SURVEYING THE BIBLE LANDSCAPE

As Vanessa thought in the first session, selecting a Bible seems like it should be a simple task, and at one point it was. But oh, how the Bible landscape has changed in the last fifty years! Let's take a look at the decisions you'll need to make in choosing a Bible to really study.

TRANSLATIONS CAN BE TRICKY

You might think you can go out and get yourself an original Bible—but that's just not possible. You will need a translation—and there are many. Here's why.

The Bible contains many books, and even the most recent of them was written almost two thousand years ago. The oldest books could have been written as early as 1500 B.C.E. as stories that had been passed on through the oral tradition—for centuries if not millennia—were written down. Most of the Bible was written in either ancient Greek or Hebrew (with a smattering of Aramaic), which are themselves different enough from modern Greek and Hebrew that they have to be learned as separate languages.

To complicate things a bit more, ancient Greek and Hebrew are considered "dead" languages. That is, no one living speaks those languages in day-to-day conversation. Unless we are schooled in those ancient languages, we have to read a translation.

The Bible today is the most translated book in the world. That is partly the work of

---

HAPAX LEGOMENA

Words that appear only once in the entire written record of a language. There are 1500 of these in the Hebrew of the Old Testament and 686 in the Greek New Testament. Translations of such words are guesses based on the context and are subject to change if and when a new cache of documents in that language is unearthed by archaeologists.

One such word in the Old Testament appears in Genesis 6:14 during the discussion of the construction of Noah's Ark. The word in question is translated "gopher wood." Scholars lean toward thinking this is a type of cypress wood, but there is no way to be certain.

Of the 686 New Testament hapax legomena, the one used most frequently in Christian faith occurs in the Lord's Prayer (in both the Matthew and Luke versions of that prayer). It is the word for "daily" in "Give us this day our daily bread." It is entirely possible that what has been translated as "daily" really means some other type of bread entirely. Pumpernickel anyone?

---

missionaries who want to be sure that the Bible is available in every language possible. But there are also so many translations within a given language because it's hard to agree on many things surrounding the translation.

One obstacle for translators is that we have no "original" biblical texts. Someday we may unearth one in the archaeological find of the millennium, but as of this moment we have only copies of copies of copies, none of which are identical. Those were hand-copied by monks and scribes with much care and sometimes with notes in the margins. Sometimes it's difficult to tell whether the marginal notes are part of the original text or not, and when two copies of the same text differ, there is often disagreement on which one to use.

A Question of Style

The Bible also contains a huge variety of literary styles and genres. It has narrative stories, allegorical parables, letters, sermons, histories, genealogies, poetry, prophecy, legal codes, census tabulations, and very, very detailed building instructions. Those differences each have their issues. For example, how do you translate ancient weights, measures, and currencies? Do you detail measurements in cubits and leave the reader to wonder how long that is? Do you convert it to feet or meters? Do you explain that it wasn't an exact measure but represented the distance between a man's elbow and the end of his middle finger? Suppose the text says that a person paid "two denarii" for something. Do you just let that stand, or do you translate it as "two days' wages" to ease understanding of the amount represented?

And how about the stylistic elements of poetry? If something rhymes in the original, should you make it rhyme in the new language to reflect the poetry of the original or should preference be given to words that are perhaps more exact but destroy the poetry? How do you reconcile translation as art and translation as science?

Psalm 23 in the King James Version of the Bible, for example, reads, "And I shall dwell in the house of the LORD forever." It is read at countless funerals. The choice of the word "forever" here is problematic, though, because the meaning of "forever" in Israel in 1000 B.C.E. was not at all what it is today. The translation that best reflects what the psalmist meant when he wrote it is, "And I shall dwell in the house of the LORD to the end of my days." But who wants to hear that at a funeral? "Forever" isn't technically wrong as a translation, but the understanding of the word has significantly changed over the millennia.

I Want to Buy a Vowel

Then there's another complicated glitch. The ancient Hebrew didn't bother to include the vowels in their written words—those didn't get added to the text until the eighth to the tenth century C.E. when a group of Hebrew scholars called the Masoretes decided that since fewer and fewer people knew ancient Hebrew, somebody had better put the vowels in before the language

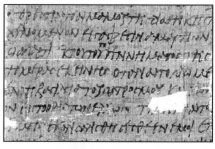

3rd or 4th century manuscript of the Gospel of Matthew

was forgotten. Did they remember correctly? Not everyone thinks so.

And then there's the business of ancient texts not bothering with modern niceties like punctuation and space between words. Neither did they have the convenient separations of chapters and verses that we now have. In the hope of making his Bible commentaries easier to use, chapters were added by Stephen Langton, a theological professor in Paris and archbishop of Canterbury in the early thirteenth century C.E. (As an aside, Langton was also instrumental in formulating the Magna Carta.)

Chapter and Verse

Dividing the chapters into numbered verses was done for the Hebrew Bible in 1448 C.E. by a rabbi philosopher named Mordecai Nathan (also known as Isaac Nathan ben Kalonymus) as a necessary tool for using the concordance that he had written—the first for the Hebrew Bible. The Latin Vulgate was given distinct verses in 1555 C.E. by Robert Stephanus (also known as Robert Etienne), who was a Protestant book printer living in France. Robert Stephanus was not the first to do this and the Bibles he printed were declared heretical. But it was his system of verse notation that was adopted in the printing of the Geneva Bible and thus became the standard in use today. Both Mordecai Nathan and Robert Stephanus used the chapter divisions of Stephen Langton. It should be noted that there is rare agreement across the theological spectrum that the chapter and verse divisions are relatively arbitrary and created for human convenience. They are not considered as divinely inspired.

CANON

In relation to the Bible, the word "canon" refers to the books of the Bible officially accepted as Holy Scripture.

Translating work like that is not for the faint of heart. "New" and "revised" versions of the Bible pop up all the time as new evidence comes to light showing that something didn't get translated quite right in an earlier version.

FOR **REFLECTION**

Have you ever studied a foreign language?

What was that experience like?

Have you ever tried to make yourself understood to someone who does not speak your language?

Have you had any experience with hearing different Bible translations? What was that like?

There are two lessons in all of that mess. First, if you meet someone who has translated the Bible from its original languages, buy her dinner. She's earned it. Second, any Bible you read already has interpretation built into it. The Masoretes who added the vowels, the people who decided where to put a comma instead of a period and who divided a verse here and not there, those who decided that we are saved by "faith *in* Jesus Christ" rather than the (equally plausible in Greek) "faith *of* Jesus Christ" (Romans 3:21–22) have made some interpretive decisions for us just in the words they chose for their translation. You will have to decide whether or not those interpretations can be trusted.

IN OTHER WORDS: TRANSLATION OR PARAPHRASE?

A translation of the Bible is the work of an individual or group who go back to the original languages of the text and attempt a word-for-word translation into English or whatever other language they are working with. Since languages have different structures, translations rearrange words or sometimes substitute words to make the sentences readable, but you can generally trace any English word back to its Greek or Hebrew original in a translation. The King James Version of the Bible goes so far as to put into italics any words not in the original languages that were added for the sake of making the English translation flow more easily.

A translation usually (but not always) is indicated by the use of the word "version" in the Bible title. For example the King James Version (KJV), the New International Version (NIV), and the New Revised Standard Version (NRSV) are all examples of popular translations. A preface will usually clear up any questions about the type of text it is, and you can even get parallel Bibles that have several translations right alongside each other.

Here's a sampling of some of the differences:

> **The King James Version (1611) translates the first three verses of Psalm 23 this way:**
>
> *The LORD is my shepherd, I shall not want. He maketh me to lie down in green pastures; he leadeth me beside the still waters. He restoreth my soul; he leadeth me in the paths of righteousness for his name's sake.*

> **The New International Version (1973) offers this translation:**
>
> *The LORD is my shepherd, I lack nothing. He makes me lie down in green pastures, he leads me beside quiet waters, he refreshes my soul. He guides me along the right paths for his name's sake.*

A *paraphrase* is generally done by one author and goes well beyond a word-for-word translation in an attempt to convey the meaning of a phrase or sentence. The best-known paraphrases of the Bible are *The Living Bible* and *The Message*.

> **The Living Bible (1971) paraphrases the same verses from Psalm 23 this way:**
>
> *Because the LORD is my Shepherd, I have everything I need! He lets me rest in the meadow grass and leads me beside the quiet streams. He restores my failing health. He helps me do what honors him the most.*

> **The Message (published in segments from 1993 to 2002) begins Psalm 23 this way:**
>
> *God, my shepherd! I don't need a thing. You have bedded me down in lush meadows, you find me quiet pools to drink from. True to your word, you let me catch my breath and send me in the right direction.*

For purposes of this study, you will need a translation. A paraphrase can be a great conversation partner and an accessible way to get a sense of meaning from a difficult passage. The Living Bible was my constant companion during my teen years, and perhaps your study group could have a paraphrase on hand just for comparison. But to truly get a sense of what the Bible is like and to be able to compare notes with others reading the same thing, get a translation.

Apart from the King James (see the box about the King James Version on the following page), the two most popular modern translations in Protestant circles are the New Revised Standard Version (NRSV), which is preferred by mainline denominations, and the New International Version (NIV), which is preferred by Evangelicals. The New American Bible (NAB) and the New Revised Standard Version (NRSV) or older Revised Standard Version (RSV) are most popular with Roman Catholics. The Orthodox prefer the Greek of the Septuagint (see Session 3, p. 35) but there is a new English translation of the Orthodox Bible called the Orthodox Study Bible.

Translation or paraphrase is only the first decision, however.

A WORD ABOUT THE KING JAMES VERSION

The King James Version (KJV) of the Bible was translated in 1611 under the authority of (surprise, surprise) King James I of England. And the first thing to note is that the translation had its origins in politics.

Adam Nicolson, author of God's Secretaries: The Making of the King James Bible[1], reminds us that King James had some intensely political reasons for ordering a new translation. The favored translation for Protestants of the day was the Geneva Bible. But in that translation, every appearance of the word "king" was translated as "tyrant." Combined with the marginal notes accompanying the Geneva Bible, it was a translation with a very definite anti-establishment view that didn't sit well with kings. The religious sectarianism in England was also fierce. King James needed a Bible translation that could unite divided religious factions while not challenging the right of kings to rule. The King James Version was the result.

Despite its political motivations, however, the King James Version is, quite simply, a masterpiece of English literature. Some would argue that it is the masterpiece of English literature. That is not to say, however, that it is easy to read. This is the period of Shakespeare and there's a reason that students today often struggle in trying to read the Bard's plays. Words and phrases that were common four hundred years ago are no longer in use, and some words that still can be heard on our streets now have a vastly different meaning.

As an example, the word "prevent" in the time of King James often meant "to allow, to make a way for." Psalm 59:10 in the KJV reads that God "shall prevent me." The New International Version, which reflects today's language, translates the same verse "God will go before me." The meaning of the passage hasn't changed, but most people reading the KJV would misunderstand because we don't use the word "prevent" in that way anymore. In fact, today it means the opposite!

The KJV is also not the most accurate translation. Discoveries in the intervening centuries have provided scholars with much more information about biblical languages and context and newer translations have the advantage of that more-informed scholarship. In its defense, the King James Version was not meant to be read and studied so much as it was meant to be heard. After the vast committee process that created the various parts of the translation, the final translation choices were not made by people looking at the pages and comparing notes. The proposed translations were read aloud to the group and were accepted or rejected based on what was heard.

Continued on next page

1 *New York: Harper Perennial, 2005.*

While it would be a shame to have the King James Version disappear from ritual use (how do you have a funeral without the KJV of the Twenty-Third Psalm or Christmas without those swaddling clothes and abiding shepherds?), the use of translations with contemporary language for personal study and devotion is much more likely to facilitate understanding.

DEVOTIONAL BIBLE OR STUDY BIBLE?

The Bibles you often find in church pews contain little more than the text and a few footnotes about translation issues. Most Bibles in retail outlets, however, contain much more, and they tend to break down into two groups.

Study Bibles. These contain lots of extra notes, charts, maps, and other study helps to assist the reader in understanding the view of scholars on various topics. A study Bible will generally have an introduction to each book that describes what is known about the book's authorship, date, and historical context. Some contain outlines of the book's contents. Typically a study Bible will contain one or more maps of areas mentioned in the Bible from different historical perspectives. Sometimes there are family trees of biblical families, glossaries of terms, and cross-references to other Bible passages related to the one you're reading.

RED-LETTER BIBLES

All kinds of Bibles and translations have red-letter options, which put the words of Jesus in red ink. However, this too is an interpretation, and scholars on both the conservative and liberal sides of the aisle are wary of it. In some cases it is quite obvious where the words of Jesus begin and end. However there are a number of places where it is not clear at all where the words of Jesus end and the commentary of the Gospel writer begins. When you have a red-letter Bible, it's easy to forget that the emphasis has been added very recently and is someone's interpretation of where Jesus' words begin and end. Again, it's not a bad thing, just something to be aware of.

A study Bible will also have large sections of footnotes to explain difficulties in translation, historical context, or cultural references. In those notes you will often learn the modern equivalents of monetary references or other forms of weights and measures. Want to know why the Temple in Jerusalem had its own currency? A note in a study Bible often will tell you.

Study Bibles tend to be similar to one another in the type of information they convey, although there are some that focus their notes on a particular type of information. The *NIV Archaeology Study Bible* is an example of this. The translation of the Bible is the NIV (New International Version) but you can expect the notes to focus on the role of archaeology in biblical understanding and research. The *Amplified Bible* takes on the daunting task of listing every possible translation for each word. That can be quite interesting, but since they are listed in the text and not in footnotes, it can make just reading a single passage a daunting task.

Devotional Bibles. These have a bit of study information, but with a fundamentally different purpose. The notes in devotional Bibles are designed to help the reader apply the Bible readings to life. Devotional Bibles tell stories and ask questions to help you reflect on what a given story or passage might be suggesting about your life now.

For that reason, there is a devotional Bible geared toward almost every existing demographic. There are those written for women, for men, for teens, for those in recovery. There are devotional Bibles that focus on particular issues, like the *Poverty and Justice Bible* and the *Green Bible*. In this latter group there is often highlighting of any biblical texts that pertain to the topic. So, for example, the *Green Bible* highlights (in green, of course) all the passages that relate to creation and the environment, while also adding introductory essays by world leaders about religion and the environment.

The notes in devotional Bibles are completely different from one another since they address different audiences. There are some devotional Bibles, like the *Life Application Bible*, that are more general in focus, but instead of notes for study of the text itself, they include commentary that's designed to get you thinking about how the text might affect your life. Both study and devotional Bibles have biases beyond what is inherent in a translation. That isn't a bad thing; it's just something to be aware of. Just because a note is printed in a Bible, doesn't mean it carries the same authority as the biblical texts themselves. The notes represent what a given scholar or group of scholars believe to be accurate or thought provoking. That's not to be sneezed at; they have studied more than you have. But they do filter their study through their own biases, as we all do.

ABOUT THE APOCRYPHA

If you're Protestant or of no particular faith, another choice that you'll make is whether to get a Bible with or without the Apocrypha (pronounced a-POK-rif-a).

The origins of this difference in the biblical canon are explained more in Session 3, page 35, but this is a set of writings included in the Roman Catholic and Orthodox canon that Protestants don't recognize as having authority equal to that of the other sixty-six books.

THE **APOCRYPHA**

The biblical books accepted in the Roman Catholic and Orthodox canon but rejected as authoritative by Protestants because they are not part of the Hebrew Scriptures.

As a Protestant clergywoman, I have always recommended that my parishioners have a Bible with the Apocrypha in it. There are some great stories and some interesting (and gruesome) history, and those who lived in the early days of Christianity were well familiar with these texts. We won't look at these books in depth in this study, but if you're going to buy a Bible, I think it's worthwhile to have the Apocrypha in there. That will, however, limit your choice of translations, as not all translations have a study Bible that includes those additional books.

BIBLE ETIQUETTE

Now that you've decided which Bible to get, let's take a look at some guidelines for using—and respecting—this special book. People often wonder about the treatment of the bound volume itself, so we'll explore the etiquette surrounding our physical treatment of the Bible.

- **The word "Bible" as a noun is always capitalized.** If you use it as an adjective, as in "biblical studies," however, it is lower case.

- **Underlining, highlighting, and making marginal notes on the pages of a Bible as you read and study is a matter of personal preference.** My approach? I have a leather-bound Bible that I use for reading only that is not marked. But I have many others that are annotated, highlighted, and marked in various ways because that helps me study. My college textbooks were the same way.

- **Using the pages of your Bible to record phone messages or doodle while you're watching TV, scribbling with the intent to deface, or putting your shopping list in the margins is disrespectful to the text.**

Suppose you have a Bible you no longer want to keep? What do you do with it? If the Bible is in good shape you can...

- See if your local church can identify someone who can use it. This is a long shot, but it doesn't hurt to check. What you should *not* do is put your unwanted Bibles in a bag and leave them on your pastor's doorstep like an abandoned baby. Ask if they can be used and if not, move to option two.

- Check with local libraries having book sales or thrift shops that sell books. Again, don't just dump them there—ask if they would be a useful addition.

- Many times people run into this situation because they are cleaning out the belongings of a loved one. If the Bible belonged to a family member, check with others in the family who might want it for sentimental reasons.

If the Bible is mildewed or moldy or falling apart or if you can't find a new recipient, then you need to make a decision.

- You can decide that no Bible should be destroyed, put it in a box and leave it for your heirs to worry about later.

- If you are part of a particular Christian tradition, ask a religious leader in that tradition if they have any rules regarding the disposition of unwanted Bibles. There is no official "Christian" rule about this but some denominations may have their own recommendations or traditions.

- You can bury it. There are some who advocate that the remains of a Bible should be treated as human remains and buried in the ground.

- You can burn it. Of course the burning of Bibles is also a sign of disrespect, but in this it is like the etiquette surrounding the flag. A public flag burning in protest can be seen as disrespect of a nation and all it stands for. And yet, when a flag is worn beyond repair, a respectful offering of that flag to the flames is exactly what is called for. A similar case can be made for Bibles.

- Try to avoid simply dumping the Bible in the local landfill, although I would argue that if this is truly your only option, God won't open the trapdoor to hell because you did it.

- Dispose of the Bible privately. Because there is no one "Christian" way to dispose of a Bible, the way you choose could be misread as disrespectful by someone else. So don't make a show of it; just do it. It's between you and God.

The "correct" way to deal with a Bible is with an attitude of reverence for the faith it represents, whatever particular action is taken. The section

> Take your new Bible and find the book of Romans in the New Testament. **Read the fourteenth chapter.**

of the Bible that I find the most instructive for these issues is Romans 14. Here St. Paul talks about all the disagreements over what Christians should or shouldn't eat, how holy days should be celebrated, and so on. Paul's guidelines? Have your heart right, he advises, and try not to be a stumbling block to others. The same principle applies to all aspects of Bible etiquette. If you opt to dispose of the Bible in some way, do so reverently and privately and you won't be wrong.

PUTTING IT ALL TOGETHER

The Bible as a single book is a construct—a collection of many, many writings that were written by different people at different times, often after a long period of having the stories told orally. Adam didn't pull out a scroll and write down his Garden of Eden adventures. Stories and histories, poems and songs were told and retold, put to music, and eventually put on papyrus and rolled up into scrolls.

In the next two chapters we'll look at how all those "books" of the Bible have been arranged and how those arrangements came to be put together in the large library we call the Bible.

PREPARATION FOR CHECK-IN

(Starting with the second class session, each meeting will begin with a ten-minute check-in during which you will each be asked to give a brief response to the following two questions. Please think about and write your responses here.)

What is one thing that was new to me in this material?

What is one question that this week's topic raises for me?

HOMEWORK
(ALL STUDENTS)

☐ Read the text for Session 3, along with each of the Bible readings listed.

☐ Think about the questions associated with each reading.

EXTRA MILE
(CEU AND CERTIFICATE STUDENTS)

☐ Pick one of the books of the Old Testament and research the question of its authorship and the time and circumstances of writing.

☐ Prepare an essay of five hundred to seven hundred words about what you discovered. Your study Bible should have information about these issues in an introduction to each book. Begin there, but also do research online or look in the introductions to other study Bibles to see if there are differences of opinion. There almost always are. What is the evidence used to determine the answers?

IT SAYS **WHAT?**

A number of Bibles have become famous for either printing errors or a particular word choice. Among my favorites are:

The Wicked Bible: This printing of the King James Version omitted the word "not" in the adultery commandment in Exodus 20:14, resulting in God commanding the Hebrews, "Thou shalt commit adultery." The printers were fined, the copies recalled, and only eleven copies are known to exist today.

The Sin-On Bible: Would-be sinners can also find solace in this 1716 printing of the King James Version in which Jesus tells the woman taken in adultery in John 8:11 to "go and sin on more" instead of to "go and sin no more."

The Printer's Bible: Given the Wicked Bible and the Sin-On Bible, this gaffe perhaps was divinely inspired. In several 1612 copies of the King James Version, Psalm 119:161 reads, "Printers have persecuted me without a cause." The word should be "princes."

The Place-makers Bible: In a printing of the second edition of the Geneva Bible in 1562, Jesus declares in Matthew 5:9, "Blessed are the placemakers: for they shall be called the children of God." It should, of course, be peacemakers. In that same printing a much worse gaffe appears in Luke 21, where the printers accidentally have Jesus condemning instead of commending a poor widow.

The Bug Bible: This one isn't an error per se, but is a product of the differences between Middle English and modern English. Myles Coverdale, who in 1535 produced the first complete printed translation of the Bible into English, rendered Psalm 91:5 as, "Thou shall not nede to be afrayed for eny bugges by night." In Middle English the word bugge doesn't mean insect but rather a ghost. The Hebrew word is *pachad*, which isn't a thing at all but rather the sense of alarm that comes from any particular thing or event. So the KJV "terror" is a better translation, but if bugs in your bed at night cause you alarm, then bugge might be the right word after all.

The Breeches Bible: In Genesis 3:7, Adam and Eve sew fig leaves together to make clothing for themselves. A 1579 translation of that verse by Whittington, Gilby, and Sampson translated what they made as "breeches." The King James Version uses "aprons." The Hebrew word can mean girdle, armor, belt, or loincloth, so really, who knows what they made? We can only be sure that they felt vulnerable (the Hebrew for naked can also mean vulnerable) and covered up.

The Owl Bible: If you were in Sunday School in 1944, there's a chance that your Sunday School teacher, reading from a King James Version printed that year, instructed girls from 1 Peter 3:5 with the words, "For after this manner in the old time the holy women also, who trusted God, adorned themselves, being in subjection to their owl husbands." The word should have been "own," but perhaps in the post-Harry Potter age, "owl husbands" has its appeal.

OVERVIEW OF THE OLD TESTAMENT

MATERIALS YOU WILL NEED FOR YOUR THIRD CLASS SESSION:

Your study Bible

Responses to the Check-in questions on page 39

Extra Mile homework if applicable

This Student Text

Pen and paper or laptop for taking notes

THE ORGANIZATION OF
THE BIBLE

The Bible begins with the creation of the universe and ends with the destruction of that universe and the establishment of a new heaven and new earth. That has led many people to believe that the Bible is organized chronologically. It isn't.

TESTAMENTS

The major divisions within the Bible are the Old and New Testaments. The word "testament" comes from the Latin *testamentum*, which means to bear witness to a formal, written agreement. Another English word that comes from the Latin *testamentum* is "testimony." Outside of religious circles, the only place you regularly hear the word "testament" today is in relation to someone's "last will and testament"—the witnessed document showing how a person would like his or her assets distributed after death. The testaments in the Bible are documents that were recorded to bear witness to the way God's people have lived out their relationships with God, with one another, and with the world in which they lived.

SUPERSESSIONISM

The view in some Christian traditions that the New Testament has greater authority and therefore "supersedes" the writing and teaching in the Old Testament. The supersessionist believes that the covenant with Israel described in the Old Testament was replaced with the new covenant with Christians described in the New Testament.

When looking at the Old and New Testaments in the Bible, you can say that *those* are arranged chronologically. "Old" in this case doesn't mean outdated; it simply means that it came first. All the material in the Old Testament (OT) was written and describes events that are earlier than any of the material in the New Testament (NT). The words *old* and *new* should not lead us to believe that the new replaces the old, but simply that the old came first and the new came later.

The Old and New Testaments could also have been called the First Witness and the Second Witness. The First Witness—the Old Testament—is the story of the people of Israel, the Jews. For that reason, the Old Testament is sometimes called the Hebrew Scriptures. That section of our Bible represents the sacred Scriptures of the Jewish faith. The New Testament bears the same kind of witness for the origins of Christianity. Sometimes the testaments are also named as the Old and New Covenants—the covenant with the Jews came first, followed by the covenant with the Christians.

It is important to remember that it was never the intention of the biblical writers to replace the Old Testament with the New. When 2 Timothy 3:16 (in the NT) says, "All scripture is inspired by God and is useful for teaching, for reproof, for correction, and for training in righteousness," the only "Scripture" in existence was the Hebrew Bible. That passage is talking about the Old Testament.

In the mid-second century C.E. a bishop named Marcion of Sinope in Asia Minor, in what is now Turkey, decided that the entire Old Testament and anything in the early Christian writings that smacked of Judaism had become irrelevant. He believed that the God of the Old Testament was a different and inferior being to the God of Jesus Christ. He issued his own collection of Scriptures based on that premise and was excommunicated and deemed a heretic. His work was one of the things that spurred the official bodies within the church to define the authoritative writings of the Bible.

Christians often forget that Christianity began as a Jewish sect. Jesus and each of his twelve main disciples were Jews. Jesus was addressed as a rabbi and taught in synagogues. Jesus was born, lived, and died a Jew. That First Witness, the Old Testament, is critical to understanding the faith of Jesus, his disciples and the world in which they lived. Those stories and histories, poems and songs, laws and proverbs were the writings that formed Jesus as a Jewish man.

The Second Witness, the New Testament, is not properly understood apart from the context of the First. That is why the Christian Scriptures include both the Old and the New Testaments. The Second Witness is an extension of, not a replacement for, the First. Apart from the Apocrypha (see p. 35), there are thirty-nine books in the Old Testament and twenty-seven books in the New for a total of sixty-six books in the Bible, written by a number of different authors in a wide variety of literary categories.

Within each of the Testaments, the books are arranged according to the type of literature they represent, or in some cases common authorship. This is true whether you are talking about the ordering of the Hebrew or the Christian Scriptures, although in the version of the Hebrew Scriptures used for Jewish worship and study the groupings have some slight differences.

For our purposes here, I will refer to the Christian grouping as the Old Testament and the Jewish grouping as the Hebrew Bible. But first, a distinction to chew on as you read.

A Word About "Truth"

Before we dive in, we need to take a deep breath and remember the culture in which we now live. We'll look at this issue again in Session 5, but along the way it will be helpful as you read to mull over the distinction between "truth" and "facts."

In the contemporary world, and especially in the contemporary Western world, we tend to think of "truth" as representing something that is factually accurate. Seems like a no-brainer, right? Here's one way that understanding has tripped me up.

When people ask about my birthday, I relate that I was born on Mother's Day. I once received a birthday greeting from a man in my congregation on May 10. I thanked him, while noting that his greeting was actually a day early—my birthday was May 11. He informed me that, no, my birthday was May 10. He had noted my age and researched when Mother's Day fell in the year I was born. He insisted that either my birthday was May 10 or I had misled the congregation by saying I was born on Mother's Day. *Mea culpa*, but let me explain.

My mother went into labor in the early evening of Mother's Day, which was indeed May 10. She did not sleep or cease her labor until I entered the world at about two in the morning on May 11. Those are the facts. To my mother, however, I was her Mother's Day gift and I was born on Mother's Day. The passing of the midnight hour and what they put on my birth certificate was immaterial to her. She well knew the facts and my birthday was correctly recorded on every form she ever filled out. But in our family narrative...in the meaning she found in my birth...the "truth" was that I was born on Mother's Day. For the man who challenged me, however, a thing had to be factual to be true and he felt misled.

From time to time in these sessions, you will be asked to reflect on what "truth" a passage might convey. When that happens (like it will in a page or two), try to put aside your twenty-first-century, post-enlightenment mindset that often equates truth only with science and verifiable fact. Try to remember that there is a very different kind of "truth" in stories and poetry and in the lived-out lives of human beings than there is in biology, physics, and the calendar in your phone.

Remember the fable Aesop told about the dog with the bone? The dog, yummy bone in mouth, sees his reflection in the water, and thinks it's another dog with another bone. Because the bone a dog has is never quite as good as the bone another dog has, Aesop's dog opens his mouth to grab the bone from the water dog. The real bone drops in the water and the dog ends up with no bone at all.

Now that story could be a factual story. It could, honestly, be a factual story about *my* dog, who would do something stupid like that before you can say "rawhide." However, the "truth" of that fable remains even if Aesop never saw such a dog or even if a dog were incapable of such an action. Because, of course, the story really isn't about dogs at all. It's about us.

As we delve into the stories of the Old and New Testaments, remember that looking to Scripture for factual truth is a relatively modern convention. For those writing the texts that came to be part of our Bible, it was the broader sense of "truth" that they sought to convey. There may well be facts in there, but that wasn't the point. It wasn't about how many calendar days passed from the creation of light to God's day of rest. It was about the "truth" that the God of Israel was the author of awesomeness and able to create order out of chaos.

You neither need nor want a fact-checker when you're reading the Bible. You want to sit at the feet of storytellers by the fire and see the truth of God and the world through their eyes. Then you are better equipped to judge whether what was "true" for them also rings "true" for you.

THE OLD TESTAMENT

The Old Testament contains thirty-nine books in four broad categories: The Pentateuch (pronounced pen-ta-tewk), History, Poetry and Wisdom Literature, and Prophets. The latter has a subdivision between the "major" and "minor" prophets. We'll look at each category in turn.

THE **PENTATEUCH**

The word *pentateuch* is Greek, meaning "five books." So, if you open your Bible and count out the first five books listed, you have this group: Genesis, Exodus, Leviticus, Numbers, and Deuteronomy.

THE PENTATEUCH: THE FAB FIVE

It's impossible to overestimate the importance of these five books, both for Jewish and Christian faith. Tradition has it that Moses is responsible for producing these books and for that reason they are often called the Five Books of Moses. In Jewish tradition, they are also called the Law or the Torah.

Both Christianity and Judaism would be unrecognizable if you took out these five books. Here you have the great stories of creation, Adam and Eve, Noah, Abraham, Jacob and his twelve sons who became the fathers of the twelve tribes of Israel, Moses and the Ten Commandments. You have the first directions for formal, communal worship, the foundation for all the kosher laws and the laws that would later comprise the Great Commandment of Jesus to love God with all your heart, soul, and strength, and to love your neighbor as yourself.

It is right that the Bible begin with these five books, since they are the foundation on which all the rest of it depends. Did Moses really write them? It depends whom you ask. Some insist he did, others insist he didn't, and you can get a sense of the reasoning from introductions and notes in your study Bible.

> **Read Genesis 1–3.**
> What important truths do these stories teach? Would those truths change if the accounts were not factual? Have you encountered these stories outside of church? What do you like about them? What questions do they raise for you?

But whatever camp you belong to, Moses is a major player in the texts themselves, from his appearance in the book of Exodus onward. More important than authorship are the stories these books tell, the laws they put forth, and the formation of a nation and a faith they describe.

These five books underlie our culture, society, and politics in ways both subtle and profound. Debates about creationism vs. evolution, questions of where it might be appropriate to post the Ten Commandments, Blue Laws about keeping the Sabbath, dietary laws, claims of land ownership in the Middle East—it all starts here in the Pentateuch.

HISTORY

The next nine books of the Old Testament are considered history. It is in these books that we encounter stories set during a time period that archaeologists and historians can study, places that can be marked on a map, and at least some people who can be identified from non-biblical, historical sources.

That is not to say, however, that this section of the Old Testament reads like a history textbook. Within the books considered "history" are some of the best stories in the Bible. This is where you will find the inspiring story of David and Goliath as well as the lusty and murderous tale of David and Bathsheba. Here is the Battle of Jericho, Elijah facing off with the prophets of Baal and then with Jezebel, and the young Samuel hearing God's voice in the still of the night.

> **Read the story of David and Goliath in 1 Samuel 17. Then read 2 Samuel 21:19 and 1 Chronicles 20:5.** What are your thoughts? What truths might the David and Goliath story be trying to teach us? Would that change if someone else killed Goliath?

In the histories, women shine in their own right more than in any other part of the Old Testament. Deborah rises to be a judge over Israel— a military as well as a political position. There is the clever Rahab who secures safety for herself and her family through political shrewdness; Queen Jezebel, who makes Cruella de Ville look saintly; and two women with entire books of their own: the faithful Ruth, a foreign-born woman who ends up being an ancestor of Jesus; and brave Queen Esther, who saves her people and whose story provides the backdrop for the Jewish festival of Purim.

But the histories are not just personal. Here is also the broad sweep of the history of a nation. Monarchies are established, land is apportioned; a country unites, then divides, then crumbles as its people are carried off into captivity by a foreign nation. There are good kings and bad kings and, ultimately, bold prophets, leaders, and craftsmen who return to rebuild Jerusalem and the Temple from ashes.

Several of these books are divided into two, with the Old Testament calling them 1 and 2 Samuel, for example. In the Hebrew Bible, however, all of the history books that the Old Testament divides are just one scroll and should be considered a unit.

READING THE **NAME OF GOD**

Many times in all Bible translations you will see the word lord, all in capital letters. You will also see the word written in regular upper- and lower-case letters, as "Lord." In Exodus 3:14, Moses learns the name of God. However that name is considered by Jews as too sacred to speak aloud. While it was written (consonants only) in the scrolls as YHWH, those reading the scrolls aloud were in a bind. What to say when the name of God appears?

They settled on the word "Lord," which in Hebrew is Adonai. That worked for the reading of the text aloud, but translators still wanted the reader to be aware of when the word "Lord" was referring to the name of God and when it was a reference to the actual word Adonai in the text. So, the convention was adopted of putting lord (in all capital letters), when the original had YHWH, and Lord (in a mix of capital and smaller letters), when the original word actually meant just the title, "Lord," which indicates a person of noble rank and authority.

TETRAGRAMMATON

It means "word with four letters" and stands for the particular four consonants (YHWH) that represent the name of God given to Moses in Exodus 3:14. That's right. God is a four-letter word.

To confuse the matter further, remember the Masoretes? They were the Hebrew scholars at the end of the first millennium C.E. who went back and added the vowels to the Hebrew Bible. Well, they had an interesting conundrum. If they put the correct vowels into the name of God, someone would be able to pronounce it and might therefore speak God's name. That was to be avoided at all costs. So the Masoretes took the Hebrew word for Lord, Adonai, and put those vowels into God's name instead. That way if you did try to pronounce it, you would be respectful...but wrong. Thus you would avoid the sin of actually speaking God's name. When you put the vowels from Adonai together with the Hebrew consonants for the name of God (YHWH) you get, in English, "Jehovah."

Most scholars today believe the original vowels would have resulted in the word "Yahweh," usually translated, "I am who I am." Since ancient Hebrew didn't distinguish between present and future tense, it could also mean, "I will be who I will be" or "I am who I will be" or "I will be who I am," or...you get the picture. Here's a question. If Moses asks God for a name and God answers, "I am who I am," is that really God's name or was it God's way of saying, "None of your business"?

Christians in a public or interfaith setting today will generally follow the Jewish custom of not speaking the name Yahweh aloud, instead using "God," "Lord," or "Jehovah" to avoid causing offense.

POETRY AND WISDOM LITERATURE

This section—Job, Psalms, Proverbs, Ecclesiastes (sometimes called Qoheleth—pronounced koh-HEL-leth—which means "teacher"), and Song of Songs (sometimes called Song of Solomon)—is the closest the Old Testament gets to the Hebrew Bible category of the Writings. All of the Poetry and Wisdom Literature falls in that Hebrew Bible category, which also includes some of what the Old Testament considers history and prophets. In this section of the Old Testament, only the book of Job does not have a traditional connection to either King David or his son, King Solomon.

If you want to know where Pete Seeger got his inspiration for the song "Turn! Turn! Turn!" popularized in the 1960s by The Byrds, you need look no further than Ecclesiastes chapter 3. Thousands of funeral mourners have been comforted by King David's Psalm 23, which refers to God as his shepherd. Proverbs are what you would expect, and Song of Songs describes the delights of physical love, which the church has usually taken as a metaphor for God's love. And of course there is poor Job, beginning and ending with a narrative about a rich man who loses everything and an unsurpassed poetic middle filled with the advice of his friends and the response of God to Job's complaint.

THE PROPHETS

In the Old Testament, the category of prophets has two subdivisions: Major Prophets and Minor Prophets. The Major Prophets consist of the books of Isaiah, Jeremiah, Lamentations, Ezekiel, and Daniel. The Minor Prophets are the remaining twelve books of the Old Testament. In fact, the Hebrew Bible places all of these latter prophets together in a category called the Twelve, which all fit on one scroll in Hebrew.

> **Read Ezekiel 37:1–14 and Isaiah 53.** What are your impressions and questions about these passages? Are any of them familiar to you? Many Christians believe that Isaiah 53 is a prediction about Jesus. Others believe this "servant" is a personification of the nation of Israel. What do you think?

The Old Testament and the Hebrew Bible differ somewhat in the identification of Major Prophets. They agree on Isaiah, Jeremiah, and Ezekiel, but the Hebrew Bible puts Lamentations and Daniel with the Writings rather than with the Major Prophets.

A word about prophecy. To contemporary ears, the word "prophecy" brings to mind Nostradamus and those who foretell the future. Biblical prophecy does include some future predictions, but that is not the prophet's primary role. A prophet in the Bible is one who speaks for God and delivers messages from God to God's people (and sometimes vice versa). Sometimes this was a message about what was coming down the pike, but more frequently it was a message from God either chastising or reassuring the people about their actions and the events happening around them.

Being a prophet was not an enviable job. Poor Jeremiah always seemed to be stuck with delivering unpleasant messages to the King. Kings don't like unpleasant messages or those who bring them, and Jeremiah spent quite a bit of time at the bottom of a muddy cistern as a result (Jeremiah 38:6).

Quite frequently the prophets conveyed God's message through object lessons. Jeremiah, for example, creates a pot and then smashes it to bits (Jeremiah 19:10-11) and buys a plot of land just as the country has been taken over and its people marched into exile (Jeremiah 32:1-15). Isaiah walks around naked and barefoot for three years (Isaiah 20). Ezekiel creates a model of the city of Jerusalem in the middle of the street and then lies down beside it for almost a year. I don't even want to tell you how God wants Ezekiel to bake his bread (Ezekiel 4:1-17).

JEREMIAD

Jeremiah is the second longest book of the Bible. Jeremiah has so many miserable messages in that extended space that it has spawned the English word jeremiad. A jeremiad is what you call a long, literary work that seems all the longer because it's tone is full of lament over the state of things, judgments about how things got that way and the prediction that the morally decrepit state of affairs will result in society's downfall—sooner rather than later. The Puritans were especially good at this. If you have just been speaking and someone calls your words a "jeremiad," you will not be invited to many parties.

Often the messages from God come to the prophet in the form of visions. Parts of Isaiah and Daniel contain such visions, full of confusing symbols and metaphors. Perhaps the most famous visions came to the prophet Ezekiel and are popularized in song. "Zekiel saw de wheel, way up in de middle of de air…" Not only did this become a popular spiritual but Ezekiel's vision of a giant wheel covered in eyes, guided by four strange creatures, is seen by some as the first recorded UFO sighting. It is also the genre of the Negro spiritual that popularized Ezekiel's vision of the Valley of Dry Bones that comes to life through the Spirit of God. "Dem bones, dem bones, dem dry bones…" A quick search on YouTube will turn up some wonderful renditions.

To label twelve books as Minor Prophets is more to speak of their length than their importance or content. This is where you find Jonah being swallowed by a whale while trying to run from God's command. In the book of the prophet

Amos (5:24) are the stirring words we remember best coming from the lips of the Rev. Dr. Martin Luther King, Jr.: "Let justice roll down like waters and righteousness like a mighty stream." And if all the confusing visions and object lessons muddle your brain about what God does and doesn't want, you can count on the "minor" prophet Micah to sum it all up: "What does the LORD require of you but to do justice, and to love kindness, and to walk humbly with your God?" (Micah 6:8)

THE APOCRYPHA OR DEUTEROCANONICAL BOOKS

To understand how this group of writings came to be set apart from the others in some traditions, we need to delve into some history and geography.

Your study Bible probably has a map that shows that while the landmass of Israel was (and still is) small, its location on the east side of the Mediterranean has always been strategic. Given the surrounding deserts, anybody who wanted to trade with the nations to the west needed access to the sea and, therefore, to the land Israel claimed for its own. Here come the invaders.

In 722 B.C.E. Assyria moved in and took the north part of the country. Then in 586 Jerusalem was sacked by the Babylonian Empire, the Temple was destroyed, and the people were taken into captivity. A good chunk of the Bible was written during this "Babylonian Captivity" or "Exile" as people reflected on what had happened to them and tried to make sense of it all. Fifty years later, under the leadership of Ezra and Nehemiah (who both have books of the Bible named for them), the Israelites were allowed to return and rebuild. The scrolls that became the Hebrew Bible were finished and solidified by Ezra during this time.

But Israel's location and strategic importance had not changed. As the power of Babylon faded, the power of Greece rose and the power of Greek culture made itself felt far and wide. Alexander wasn't called "the Great" for nothing, and his conquests around 330 B.C.E. ensured that both Greek culture and Greek language flourished wherever he went. In Israel, Hebrew began to be heard less and less and Greek flowed from Israelite lips more and more.

The Septuagint Or LXX

Now religious leaders had a problem. People were less and less able to understand their own sacred texts, which were written primarily in Hebrew. This was especially true for Jews living outside of Palestine, where the Greek language reigned supreme. To address this need, some seventy or so scholars began work on a Greek translation of the Hebrew Bible in Alexandria sometime during the third century B.C.E. They produced the Septuagint.

SEPTUAGINT

The Greek translation of the Hebrew Scriptures. The translation was named the *Septuagint* (pronounced sep-TOO-a-jint), which means seventy in Greek, representing the approximate number of scholars who worked on the translation. Tradition has it that each of these scholars worked independently and that each one produced the exact same translation, thus confirming God's hand in the work and the reliability of the translation. Thus it is also often referred to with the Roman numerals for seventy, LXX.

The popularity—and the scope—of the Septuagint grew, however, and by 132 B.C.E. it included some additional writings that were not in the collection brought together by Ezra. These "extra" books were newer, Jewish writings from the Second Temple period (530 B.C.E. to 70 C.E.). These writings were of interest to Jews, but were not accepted as part of the canon of the Hebrew Bible.

Because they were not in the Hebrew Bible, but only in the Septuagint, they became known as "hidden" books and in Greek that translates to "*apocrypha*." What to do with them? Christians had been using them as sacred texts from the beginning due to their inclusion in the Septuagint.

Many early Christian communities disputed the Jewish conclusion that these books were not to be considered part of the canon and continued to see and use the Apocrypha as part of Scripture. And why wouldn't they? They themselves were circulating "new" sacred texts. They had letters from Peter and Paul, all sorts of stories of the life of Jesus, and their own early history that provided nourishment for their souls and guidance for their lives.

A Solution

By 70 C.E. there was a new world super-power, Rome, and its official language, Latin. Eventually a Latin Bible translation was needed, and in the fourth and fifth centuries C.E., a Christian priest named Jerome provided it. His translation was known as the Vulgate (from the Latin for "language of the people") and included New Testament texts as well. Jerome was later canonized for his efforts. Jerome did his Old Testament translation from the Hebrew Bible and not the Septuagint, so he had a decision to make. What to do with these "extra" books known as the Apocrypha?

Jerome took a middle road. He did not believe they should be considered part of the Bible, per se, but he did believe they were valuable. Other Christian leaders of the time thought they should be part of the Bible without reservation. So, he compromised. He included them in the Vulgate, but he separated them out in their own section. And so the Apocrypha sat in the Bibles of the church for the next thousand years, accepted by many as divinely inspired and questioned by others.

Those Pesky Protestants

When the Protestant reformers came along in the sixteenth century, however, the debate over these books was reignited. Believing the Hebrew Bible to be closer to the "original" than the Septuagint, the Protestants joined the Jews in refusing the authority of the contested books. Martin Luther kept them out of his German translation and eventually most Protestant translations took the Apocrypha out as well. Catholic and Orthodox churches, however, kept them (with a few small differences between the two traditions), and that is still the general rule. Roman Catholic and Orthodox churches refer to these books as *Deuterocanonical*, meaning "second canon." The original 1611 version of the King James included the Apocrypha, although it is difficult to find a later version of the KJV that has retained it.

In the late twentieth century there came to be more interest in the Apocrypha in Protestant circles. After all, the Septuagint was in broad use among Jews in first-century Palestine, so both Jesus and Paul would have known those stories and perhaps considered them sacred. Now you can find some Protestant translations that include the Apocrypha—as Jerome included it—in a separate section.

> ## IN A **NUTSHELL**
>
> ***Apocrypha***: (capital A) The word Protestants use for the contested books and stories of the Septuagint.
>
> ***Deuterocanonical***: The word Catholic and Orthodox traditions use for the contested books and stories of the Septuagint.
>
> ***Pseudepigrapha***: The word all Christian traditions use for ancient books about biblical people and events that are not formally accepted into the canon of any Christian tradition.
>
> ***apocryphal***: (small a) A word that is interchangeable with pseudepigraphic.
>
> ***Confused***: How most people who read these definitions feel.

The Apocrypha includes some great stories, some additions to the books of Daniel and Esther, letters, prayers, and large swaths of history that give the reader a sense of what was happening in Israel during the two hundred years prior to the birth of Jesus. They are definitely worth reading. Did God inspire them? You'll have to decide that for yourself.

One last note. The books of the Apocrypha are not the only books that have been debated. There are other writings from both the Old Testament and New Testament periods that different sects, individuals, and traditions have claimed belong in the body of the Bible. In an uninspired moment, someone decided that these books should be dubbed "apocryphal," making an issue that was already confusing even more so.

Then, in an act of lexicographal one-upmanship, such additional books are sometimes also called pseudepigraphic or even the Pseudepigrapha (which means "false writing" in Greek). Pull that out at a party when you're eager to lose your current conversation partner.

The thing to remember is that the books and passages actually printed in some Bibles today comprise the Apocrypha (capital A). You will never find books that are simply "apocryphal" printed in the same bound volume as the rest of the Bible. But you will certainly find them printed separately and available online.

> **Read the book of Susanna.** If you have the Apocrypha in a separate section of your Bible (Protestant), you can find it there. If the Apocrypha is integrated into the text (Roman Catholic or Orthodox), this story is the thirteenth chapter of Daniel. If your Bible does not contain the Apocrypha at all, do an online search for "Susanna apocrypha." You can read the text there—it's only one chapter. If you were deciding, would you include that story in the Bible? Why or why not?

You can find them in collections with titles like *The Gnostic Gospels*, *The Other Bible*, and *The Nag Hammadi Scriptures*, or by their individual names. The Gospel of Thomas, the Gospel of Mary, Paul and Thecla, the Apocalypse of Peter, and the Shepherd of Hermas are all examples of writing in this category.

To declare such works "apocryphal" (small a) or "pseudepigraphic" is not to say that there is no truth in them. A number of them have considerable overlap with stories in the canonical books of the Bible. It is simply to say that no official Christian bodies have been convinced that they should be declared authoritative.

PREPARATION FOR CHECK-IN

(*Prepare for the next group session by thinking about and writing a brief response to these two questions.*)

What is one thing that was new to me in this material?

What is one question that this week's topic raises for me?

HOMEWORK
(ALL STUDENTS)

☐ Read the text for Session 4, along with each of the Bible readings listed.

☐ Think about the questions associated with each reading.

EXTRA MILE
(CEU AND CERTIFICATE STUDENTS)

☐ Research the letters known as the Pastoral Epistles (1 and 2 Timothy and Titus) and prepare a five-hundred-word written report contrasting the arguments both for and against Paul's authorship of these letters.

OVERVIEW OF THE
NEW TESTAMENT

MATERIALS YOU WILL NEED FOR YOUR FOURTH CLASS SESSION:

Your study Bible

Responses to the Check-in questions on page 53

Extra Mile homework if applicable

This Student Text

Pen and paper or laptop for taking notes

AND NOW FOR SOMETHING COMPLETELY DIFFERENT

The divisions of the New Testament are not quite as standardized as those of the Old Testament, but the differences don't really cause issues. There are the four Gospels, which tell of the life of Jesus, one book of history (Acts of the Apostles), a pile of letters, and then the final Apocalypse (Revelation).

Some divisions put the Gospels with Acts and call it all history, and most groupings separate the various letters, but not all in the same way. The most common way to divide the letters is to separate out the letters of Paul and the letters of everybody else. There are a number of scholars who question whether some of the letters attributed to Paul are really his, so the list of books under a category called Paul's Letters can be different depending on where you look.

The letters that everyone agrees are *not* written by Paul are Hebrews; James; 1 and 2 Peter; 1, 2, and 3 John; and Jude. They are usually called "general letters."

Unlike the Old Testament, which very literally spans millennia, the New Testament covers a period of only fifty to sixty years. The decisions about which books would be included and which would not were made centuries after the events described rather than millennia afterward, as was the case with the Hebrew Bible. In the formation of the New Testament, there wasn't time for long-term historical reflection on the events described, so you don't have the kinds of sweeping historical books that you do in the Hebrew Bible. The New Testament is more immediate, encompassing the writings about the life of Jesus, the very earliest accounts of the Christian movement (begun as a Jewish sect called the Way), letters to both churches and individuals, and a pretty wild prophetic vision at the end. Let's look at each of the groups of books that comprise the New Testament.

GOSPELS AND THE ACTS OF THE APOSTLES

The word "gospel" comes from the Old English *god-spell* (thus the Broadway musical about Jesus by that name) and means "good news."

SYNOPTIC **GOSPELS**

Matthew, Mark, and Luke.

The word "synoptic" means to see things in a similar way. The first three Gospels are very similar in content and style. Since the Gospel of John is so different, the first three are often grouped together under this heading.

The Greek word is *evangelion* and it occurs seventy-six times in the New Testament. In literary terms,

> **Read the parable of the Prodigal Son in Luke 15:11–32.**

the word Gospel refers to writing about the life and teaching of Jesus. There were many, many gospels written but only four made it into the official compilation we call the New Testament: Matthew, Mark, Luke, and John. It is generally assumed that the Gospel of Mark is the earliest of the four and that the other three writers had access to it when they wrote their accounts.

Matthew, Mark, and Luke each address their gospels to different constituencies, and they choose to include different stories or to emphasize different ideas or events. But they read in a similar way and the timeline of Jesus' life is roughly the same. For that reason, those three gospels are called the "Synoptic Gospels"—from *syn* (same) *optic* (see).

The Gospel of John is a whole different kettle of fish. John is the last of the gospels to have been written, probably by a

> **Read John 1:1–18.** This is all you get of Christmas in John.

good many years. It is likely that John had not only Mark to look at but Matthew and Luke as well. It has often been suggested that John is more like a commentary on the other gospels—that while the first three gospels tell us what Jesus did and what he said, John tells us what it all means. John is deeper and more philosophical than the other gospels. The ordering of events is different and there is layer upon layer of meaning.

Luke also deserves special mention because of its relation to the book of Acts. Most scholars agree that Luke (possibly a Greek physician who traveled with Paul) wrote both Luke and Acts. In fact, you'll sometimes see reference to just one book called Luke-Acts. In antiquity you could fit thirty sheets of papyrus into a single scroll. Luke fills thirty sheets, the assumption being that the only reason we have two books (Luke and Acts) instead of one is because Luke ran out of scroll.

In fact, the beginning of Acts is a continuation of the life of Jesus recorded in Luke, and it is addressed to the same person

> **Read Acts 9:1–19.** The story of Saint Paul's conversion.

(Theophilus) and mentions the author's "first" book. Acts begins with the ascension of the resurrected Jesus into heaven before it moves on to tell of the lives of the disciples after Jesus was gone.

Christ enthroned amongst the Four Evangelists, from the Codex Bruschal, c. 1220

A "disciple" is one who learns from a master. An "apostle" is one who is sent out on a mission. In the book of Acts, we see the disciples from the gospels come to the end of their training with Jesus. Then the narrative turns to show how they are transformed into apostles and sent out to spread that gospel—the good news that they learned from him. Acts shows us how the early church was begun, how those who were not Jews got

into the act, and how a Pharisee named Saul (whose name is later changed to Paul), who actively persecuted the first Christians, became one of Christianity's most ardent defenders.

The four Gospels in our New Testament were the second set of writings (after the letters of Paul) to be collected together and deemed authoritative. It wasn't an easy process. An early Christian writer and theologian from Assyria named Tatian didn't like the thought of having several "different" gospels put out there, so in 170 C.E. he tried putting Matthew, Mark, and Luke together in one cohesive narrative with some other bits of oral tradition thrown in. It didn't gain any traction, and by the end of the second century, it was accepted that we had a "four-fold gospel," comprised of four books. Each piece of the single "four-fold gospel" tells the narrative of Jesus' life according to the perspective of a given writer. So today you see the Gospel "according to Matthew" or the Gospel "according to Mark," and so on.

LETTERS

Paul was a Pharisee—someone who was trained in and who interpreted Jewish law. He was an educated man and con-

> **Read I Corinthians 13:1–13.**
> The nature of love.

sidered himself a Jew, even after he became a follower of Jesus. Paul was literate, learned, and zealous. Probably he was difficult to live with, but his fierce determination to tell the world about Jesus and his resurrection from the dead lit a fire under all of Asia Minor—modern-day Turkey—as well as parts of Greece and even Rome as he traveled and founded churches in place after place.

The Acts of the Apostles is largely devoted to his story, and much of the rest of the New Testament is comprised of the letters he wrote to both the churches he founded and the pastors he sent to care for them as he moved from one community to another. Paul is a love-him-or-hate-him kind of guy, but there is no denying his prominence, both in the New Testament and in the founding of the early church.

Paul's letters were the first writings of the New Testament to be gathered together in a collection and were most probably the first books of the New Testament written in their completed form. At the beginning of the second century C.E., ten of Paul's letters were grouped together as a set of authoritative writing: Romans, 1 and 2 Corinthians, Galatians, Ephesians, Philippians, Colossians, 1 and 2 Thessalonians, and Philemon. The earliest of Paul's letters were written about 50 C.E., with many claiming the first was Galatians and others claiming it was 1 Thessalonians. Both were written close to that time.

The letter to Titus and the two letters to Timothy are often dubbed the "Pastoral Epistles," and weren't as readily accepted. By the end of the second century, however, they were recognized as authoritative

> **Read 1 Timothy 4:1-16.**
> Words to encourage a young pastor.

for the church, although the question over whether Paul actually wrote them is still a matter of debate among scholars. Likewise the letter to the Hebrews, whose author is unknown, gained its acceptance in that same late-second-century time frame.

Paul was the most prolific letter writer of the New Testament, but he was not the only one. The letters of Peter, John, James, Jude, and whoever wrote Hebrews fill out the picture with a variety of perspectives. Most of these

> **Read James 2:14-26.**
> Faith and works.

"general letters" (sometimes called the "catholic epistles" because they were written to all churches rather than a particular congregation) weren't readily included into the New Testament.

It wasn't universal, but most Christian communities accepted 1 Peter and 1 John during the second and third centuries. However, James, 2 Peter, 2 and 3 John, and Jude were way down on the list and parts of the church were still rejecting them as late as the sixth century. Even as late as the sixteenth century C.E., Martin Luther had to be arm-twisted to include James in his German translation of the Bible.

Another book that Martin Luther (and those earlier Christians who didn't like many of the general letters) would sooner have left out of the Bible is Revelation. Many Christians today would like to remove it as well. This book of the Bible is responsible for some of the most beautiful things in American culture, yet some would say it is also responsible for some of the oddest.

APOCALPYTIC **LITERATURE**

In the Bible, these are books or parts of books that are characterized by their focus on the upheaval and destruction of the world or a given civilization. They are often relayed in highly symbolic language coming from the writer's dreams or visions, and are frequently written during times of persecution or extreme difficulty.

Revelation represents a genre of literature that we saw a bit of in the Old Testament. It is called apocalyptic. The Greek word *apocalypse* means "revelation," thus the book's title. It represents a prophetic vision of a time to come that relies heavily on symbolic language. The Old Testament contains quasi-apocalyptic literature in portions of Isaiah, Jeremiah, Joel, and Zechariah, plus a full-blown apocalypse in the book of Daniel.

In American culture, the book of Revelation shows up in two primary ways. One is in the "Hallelujah Chorus" of Handel's *Messiah*, which is from Revelation 11:15; 19:6; and 19:16. The "Worthy Is the Lamb" chorus in the *Messiah* can also be found there, in Revelation 5:12–13.

In the twentieth century, however, more people became familiar with Revelation as a horrifying picture of the end times: the Four Horsemen of the Apocalypse (shown on the following page), the Mark of the Beast, 666, people being "left behind" in the rapture (even though the passages that comprise the basis for the rapture are not in the book of Revelation), and a multi-million-dollar business in scaring people into thinking we are living in the end times.

Radio broadcaster Harold Camping made over $70 million by claiming that he had cracked the code of Revelation and knew the end of the world would be May 21, 2011. Even though he had already unsuccessfully predicted such an end on May 21, 1988 and on September 7, 1994, people believed him and sent him money to promote his message. He was not the first such opportunist and he will not be the last.

Four Horsemen of the Apocalypse, ca. 1497-98, Albrecht Dürer

The book of Revelation begins innocently enough, with seven letters from God to seven churches in seven locations around Asia Minor. They reference sects and heresies that we can only speculate about today but otherwise are pretty straightforward and are helpful reminders of the priority God should have in the lives of the faithful.

Next come several chapters of praise as the vision shifts to a scene in heaven of God surrounded by all sorts of creatures engaged in worship and Jesus in a prominent place. A lot of this section is poetry and some of it can be found in hymns as well as classical music.

The Antichrist And Conspiracy Theories

Then it gets strange. The vision shifts to angels who pour out bowls of disasters on the earth, and earthly events are described in terms of multi-horned beasts, whores, and some kind of evil mark you must have to buy or sell anything. A friend who worked in a Christian bookstore in Georgia reported that a customer returned a whole pile of books she had bought the day before. The reason for the return? She was aghast to find that books she had bought—from a Christian bookstore, mind you—bore the mark of the beast. The mark? The UPC barcode.

I don't doubt that the woman was sincere in her faith, but she had been duped into looking for signs of the end at every turn. I feel for her. I was swept up in that kind of thinking in my earlier years and became so caught up in looking for the end times that I was very little good in the present.

And then there's 666—the number of the beast. Revelation 13:18 practically begs for people to run wild with this. The verse reads, "This calls for wisdom: let anyone with understanding calculate the number of the beast, for it is the number of a person. Its number is six hundred sixty-six." Never mind that some ancient manuscripts have 616; the 666 is what has stuck. And who doesn't want to be considered wise? Everyone wants to be the person who figures it out.

> **HEXAKOSIOIHEXEKONTAHEXAPHOBIACS:**
>
> The term for people with a debilitating fear of the number 666.

Every time things get bad, people begin to wonder if this is it. Paul thought the end times were so close to his day that he advised people not even to get married. (1 Corinthians 7:8) And it has been that way ever since. When some-one rises to prominence, those who hate him figure out a way to work the numbers so that his name equals 666. It's been going on for centuries.

Nero has been identified as the Antichrist, as have any number of popes and even the papal office itself. Of course it was done for Hitler, Mao Zedong, Stalin, and even for tyrants in general. As US politics became more partisan, Ronald Reagan got the treatment (full name: Ronald Wilson Reagan; each of his three names has six letters) as well as every subsequent US president. Henry Kissinger, various General Secretaries of the United Nations, and Bill Gates can be made to fit the number. Someone even did it for Barney the Dinosaur. Take "Cute Purple Dinosaur," take out all the letters that are not Roman numerals (converting the u's to v's), convert those to Arabic values and then add them up. That's right. 666.

It's Supposed To Be Hopeful

There are a number of scholars who believe the predictions of the time of tribulation in Revelation were predictions of the fall of

> **Read Revelation 21:1–6.**
> The New Jerusalem.

Rome—and that event is over and done with. Of course many see it as a time yet to come. What gets lost in all of that is that the message of Revelation is meant to be one of hope. The book ends with a new heaven and a new earth, lit by the glory of God. It was written to a people undergoing fierce and terrible persecution, who needed to know that God heard their cries and that there would be justice for those who were cruelly murdering them and their families solely because they would not bow to the Roman emperor as god.

What comfortable twenty-first-century Americans see as a time of terror and a chance for conspiracy theories, the original, persecuted recipients cheered as a promise of justice, just as there was literally dancing in the streets of the United States when Osama bin Laden was killed. Other parts of the Bible warn us against rejoicing in the destruction of our enemies, and Revelation does not encourage that. But it's understandable that those who were dipped in tar and set aflame to light Emperor Nero's garden might appreciate a God who was fighting mad about it.

FORMING THE CANON:
BIBLE BY COMMITTEE

After a few centuries had passed since the life of Jesus, later generations of Christians had to finally decide which writings would be considered official and included in their sacred Scriptures—and which would not. It was a complicated process. Those writings that were seen as representing those who had direct knowledge of the events or had been with Jesus either directly or indirectly tended to carry more weight, as did writings addressed to the entire church. Over time, these came to be valued above the others. Of course it was only a matter of time before someone asked, "Are you *sure* John (or whoever) wrote this?" and then the debate about the official canon (from a Greek word meaning "measure" or "rule") was off and running. What books would comprise the canon, or rule, for Christian faith?

We've seen that over the first few centuries C.E., at least basic agreement began to coalesce around certain collections of writings. As we also have seen, however, there was disagreement among various Christian communities about which writings should be accepted as authoritative. There were many, many other writings out there and you can find them in a variety of collections today. Plus, there were church leaders like Marcion taking the matter into their own hands and expunging references to the Hebrew Scriptures from New Testament writings.

Not to be outdone, in 367 C.E., the bishop of Alexandria, Athanasius, sent out an Easter letter in which he named the twenty-seven books we have today as the "canon" of the New Testament. His listing enjoyed a much better reception than that of Marcion, but it still did not settle the matter in all sectors and a number of councils were held in ensuing centuries to try to keep the debate down to a dull roar.

By the fifth century, acceptance of those twenty-seven books listed by Athanasius was pretty much universal, but it wasn't firmly settled until the Council of Trent (1546) for Roman Catholics, the Thirty-Nine Articles (1563) for the Church of England, the Westminster Confession of Faith (1647) for Calvinism, and the Synod of Jerusalem (1672) for the Eastern Orthodox Church.

It's important to remember that when you encounter a reference to "Scripture" in the New Testament (as in 2 Timothy 3:14–17), the writer is referring to the Hebrew Bible. There was no "New Testament" at that point. What you had were prominent figures in the early church recording events or sending letters to fledgling Christian communities for a variety of purposes.

FOR **REFLECTION**

Does knowing how the Bible was put together make you think about it differently? In what way?

Does this issue raise any questions for you?

Does it settle any questions for you?

What do you suppose it was like sitting in on a council that was deciding on the canon of Scripture?

PREPARATION FOR CHECK-IN

(Prepare for the next group session by thinking about and writing a brief response to these two questions.)

What is one thing that was new to me in this material?

What is one question that this week's topic raises for me?

HOMEWORK
(ALL STUDENTS)

☐ Re-read the section titled "A Word About 'Truth'" from Session 3 (p. 28).

☐ Read the text for Session 5, along with each of the Bible readings listed.

☐ Think about the questions associated with each Bible reading.

☐ Think about the questions under "Your Own Beliefs" on page 65.

EXTRA MILE
(CEU AND CERTIFICATE STUDENTS)

☐ Look at the questions for reflection with the Jonah reading on page 62 and, in five hundred to seven hundred words, write a response.

☐ Be prepared to lead a discussion of those questions during Session 5.

THE **BIBLE** AND ITS **AUTHORITY**

MATERIALS YOU WILL NEED FOR YOUR FIFTH CLASS SESSION:

Your study Bible

Responses to the Check-in questions on page 66

Extra Mile homework if applicable

This Student Text

Pen and paper or laptop for taking notes

BUT THE BIBLE SAYS...

This probably doesn't come as news to you, but people get into arguments about the Bible all the time, even within the Christian community. There are debates aplenty about a host of issues, from presidential politics to elementary education, with all sides pulling out the Bible to make their case for their favorite position.

Of course, many people find themselves with a particular view simply because someone they trust told them that's how it was. It is important in our intellectual and spiritual formation to know what we believe, but to truly claim authentic belief, we also need to know *why* we believe what we do (or don't). Ideally, we also listen to others tell us why *they* believe certain things and then we put it together with our own experiences and thoughts to make up our own minds. Then, and only then, is a belief truly our own.

Behind all the arguing about the Bible are two central tensions: First, what role did God play in the creation of the Scriptures? And second, what authority or relevance does the Bible have for our lives today? If you have been doing the reading and class exercises in Sessions 1–4, you already may be asking yourself those very questions. This session seeks to help you think through those issues.

THE CONTINUUM

If you approached twelve different people and asked them, "What role did God play in the creation of the Bible?" chances are you would get eleven different answers and one blank stare. The same holds true for the question of the Bible's authority. These are not yes or no questions for most people. The "answers" represent a continuum of belief with absolute positions on each end of the line, but with most people having a more nuanced approach, placing them in other locations along the spectrum.

The matter gets further complicated by the fact that the two questions overlap in significant ways. For instance, if I believe that God played an active role in the creation and preservation of the Bible, I am much more likely to see the Bible as having significant authority and relevance in daily life.

The chart at the end of this session represents the various ways that these questions influence each other, and your main task in this session is to think about your current beliefs and perhaps actually plot them on the chart. Doing so does not mean you will never change your mind or move in a different direction, but being able to identify what you believe now, at least to some extent, will help you engage others in dialogue more effectively.

Before we get to the actual chart, however, let us look at the two questions in light of the absolute positions that can be found at the ends of each spectrum.

THE ABSOLUTES

WHAT ROLE DID GOD PLAY IN THE CREATION OF THE BIBLE?

The two absolute poles related to this question are:

- God as the **sole author**, dictating the Bible word for word to human beings who were protected by God from introducing any error of any sort into the text. For the purposes of discussion, we'll call this the "Sole Author" position.

- The Bible as a completely **human work**, subject to both human bias and error, in which God played no role at all beyond being the subject about which people wrote. We will refer to this position as "Human Work."

Now let's look at these two absolute positions in more detail.

SOLE AUTHOR

Those who see the Bible as devoid of any error of any type (a position often referred to as "inerrancy") tend to arrive at that conclusion because they believe God had a direct hand in crafting every moment of human history, including the

> **God Said it.**
> **I Believe it.**
> **That Settles it.**

writing and preservation of the writings that became our Bible. In this view, there is only one biblical author, and that is God. Those who put pen to paper had such a direct connection to the Divine that they became incapable of conveying any sort of error—religious, scientific, historical, social, or any other kind. God spoke and the writers wrote it down, just as God intended it.

If God said that 10,000 men marched into battle, then that's how many there were. Not 10,001 and not 9,999—there were 10,000.

This view has God speaking in every verse for all time. There is no historical context that would make the text require interpretation, no personal bias of the author or the author's community that would slip in. No part of the Bible truly contradicts any other—it is all the same truth of God—and if there should be *seeming* contradictions, it just highlights our need for more information. The plain meaning of the text is there for all to see. It is what it is and it says what it says, and that's that. The Bible is completely and totally inerrant, even (for some) in translation.

In this group are what have been dubbed the "young-earth creationists," who believe that the days of creation in Genesis 1 refer to twenty-four-hour time periods and, when combined with the number of generations listed in the genealogies, calculate that the earth is a mere six thousand years old.

HUMAN WORK

We learned in science class that for every action there is an equal and opposite reaction, so what lies at the opposite end of this spectrum about God's role is no surprise. For this group, God had no part at all in the creation of the books that became our Bible. It is, in their eyes, a purely human creation and God didn't provide so much as a cup of coffee for those who labored over its pages.

Of course atheists would fall into this view of the Bible by definition, since they don't believe there is a God to create, inspire, or even offer editorial suggestions. But there are also people of faith who have simply decided that working in and through human authors in any way is simply not how God operates.

This position does not necessarily imply that the Bible has no authority or relevance, however. Remember that while these questions have overlap, they are distinct questions. Many in this category recognize the impact of the Bible on culture and the arts or find the teachings of Jesus or the calls to justice made by the prophets to be worthy of consideration and even emulation. They simply believe that the source of such relevance and authority is solely human and therefore prone to errors, contradictions, primitive moral structures, and political self-justification.

WHAT AUTHORITY DOES THE BIBLE HAVE IN DAILY LIFE?

The two absolute poles related to this question are:

- The Bible is a **rulebook** that should be consulted and has a solution for every problem and circumstance in both private and public life. We will refer to this pole as "The Rulebook."

- The Bible is an **ancient relic** that has no contemporary application or authority. This position we will call the "Ancient Relic."

Now let's examine them in more detail.

THE RULEBOOK

This group is comprised of those who believe that the answer to every single question in life can be found somewhere in the Bible. It's a rulebook that trumps every law of every nation or organization. Those who believe in God as Sole Author often overlap with this group at least to some extent. After all, if you think God dictated all the biblical laws and there is no chance that they contain any human error, bias, or historical limitation—well, you'd be hard-pressed not to follow them to the letter.

There is also a tendency here to see *every* passage in the Bible as indicative of some kind of law or rule. Certainly there are laws aplenty, as we saw in Session 3. But this group will generally go beyond the explicit laws and see biblical narratives, Psalms, and other genres of literature in the Bible as containing at least hints and clues to the rules by which God wants us to live. An example of that would be in referencing the poetry of Psalm 139:13b, "You knit me together in my mother's womb" as guidance for the issue of abortion.

The Rulebook position, however, faces a question that those in the Sole Author camp do not. What do you do with things the Bible doesn't mention? Some believe that if the Bible doesn't specifically forbid something, it is permissible. Others believe all that is allowed are those things specifically permitted in the pages of the Bible.

An example of the latter can be found in the area of music in the Church of Christ denomination. The Church of Christ does not allow for instrumental music, but does include the singing of hymns in their worship. Two things are at play here. The first is that they see only the New Testament as an authoritative rulebook. That eliminates all the harps and lyres, tambourines and

Protester displaying Ten Commandments.

trumpets of the Old Testament. The second is their belief that if the New Testament doesn't mention a given practice, it is forbidden. After the Last Supper, Jesus and his disciples are recorded as having sung a hymn before they left. That allows for singing. However, there are no musical instruments mentioned in New Testament worship, so they are excluded.

ANCIENT RELIC

Those who hold this absolute position might look at the Bible and say "ancient relic" with the love and curiosity of the archaeologist or with the disdain of someone who despises all it stands for. Either way, they share a belief that whatever the Bible is, it is not to be used as an authority either in private or public life and has nothing helpful to say to contemporary ears.

As with the Sole Author and Rulebook positions, there is often overlap between those who view the Bible as a solely human work and those who believe it is an ancient relic, but there are distinctions to be made. Just as those who see the Bible as a human work would allow for some human works (including laws) to have authority and relevance, so those who see the Bible as an ancient relic might still hold out for some role that God could play.

There are those who view the Bible as containing divine inspiration of some kind but for a different era in time or for a different group of people. There are those who believe it has authority for those who choose to accept it, but not for themselves. Still others believe that God is always doing something new and that the old is, therefore, to be discarded or only viewed as a relic of a past faith, even if the originals came from the very mouth of God.

DISPENSATIONALISM

An example of this last position is found in the group of evangelical Christians who adhere to dispensationalism, a system that divides human history into a number of distinct ages or dispensations (typically seven), each with its own set of expectations and promises. While the distinction of different eras or ages of God's activity was present in antiquity, dispensationalism was systematized in the nineteenth century by a Plymouth Brethren minister named John Nelson Darby, and it is his system that provided the foundation for the scenarios of the end of the world so prevalent in books and films like the Left Behind series.

Because in Darby's system the age of the church doesn't begin until Pentecost (fifty days after Easter), all the teachings of Jesus fall into a prior age and only have authority for that age. Those who rely more deeply on the teachings of Saint Paul than the teachings of Jesus are often dispensationalists.

> **Read the Old Testament book of Jonah**
> (it's only four chapters long) and, remembering the thoughts on the nature of truth and facts from Session 3 (p. 28), reflect on the following questions: Think of a fable/story you have heard that was fiction but conveyed an important truth. What was true and not true in that fable/story? What does it mean for something to be true? What is the difference between facts and truth? What do you think it means to say the Bible is true?

THE MODERATES

Of course most people, including most Christians, do not find themselves in any of those absolute categories, although each of us probably leans toward some of them and away from others.

For example, one of the things I learned in doing ecumenical work was that Catholics and Protestants use the word "inerrant" differently. When Protestants claim an "inerrant" view, they usually mean that the Bible contains no errors of any type, as we discussed in the previous section. It is an absolute position. When Catholics use the term, however, they mean to say that the books of the Bible are without error *in the matters that God was intending to address.*

With the Catholic view, you have some room for scientific and historical inaccuracies and contradictions, because God was not thought to be writing a textbook for those subjects. God is conveying religious, moral, and spiritual truth in the Bible and it is those matters and those alone that remain above error. In fact, the Pontifical Biblical Commission in 1993 stated that, "fundamentalism [by which they mean the Protestant view of inerrancy] actually invites people to a kind of intellectual suicide." [2]

Once you leave the absolute positions on our two questions about God's role and the Bible's authority, each question tends to have a term that defines the long sliding scale between the poles. For the question about God's role in the creation of the Bible, that word is "inspiration."

---

2 *Pontifical Biblical Commission, "The Interpretation of the Bible in the Church," (document prepared for Pope John Paul II, presented March 18, 1994 with preface by Cardinal Joseph Ratzinger). Available online at catholic-resources.org/ChurchDocs/ PBC_Interp.htm.*

INSPIRATION

Those who speak of the Bible as "inspired" believe that human beings definitely wrote the Bible (i.e. it was not strict dictation from God), and those human authors might have included their own agendas, biases, and factual inaccuracies. The language of inspiration makes room for biblical contradiction and errors, both in the original writings and in translation. Of course the assumed degree of those errors and biases would determine whether a person was closer to the Sole Author absolute or the Human Work at the other end of the spectrum.

For those who speak of inspiration as it relates to the Bible, God is present and active in its creation, but not solely responsible for its contents. In some indefinable way, God "inspired" the biblical writers to record events, stories, poetry, teaching, and all the rest to show us what faithfulness has looked like in a variety of times and places. From that, we can take what is applicable to our own lives and create our own version of faithfulness.

When people use the word "inspired" about the Bible, they mean that it is more than just any old book. It is sacred—perhaps in a way that can't quite be defined, but sacred nonetheless. God is saying something in its pages—or at least in some of the pages.

PRINCIPLES

When it comes to our second question, "What authority does the Bible have in daily life?" the term that dominates the sliding scale is "principles." Where the absolutes see hard and fast rules that should be applied literally and in the same way across time and space, those elsewhere along the line talk more of guiding principles and moral examples.

People here begin to look at many biblical specifics as being bound to the time or culture in which they were written but still see in them a general moral code that should have authority for contemporary life.

For example, take the law from Deuteronomy 25:4, which reads, "Do not muzzle an ox while it is treading out the grain." For the absolute position, this means nothing if you don't have an ox. It is about muzzling an ox and only an ox and only if it is treading grain. If your ox is treading grapes or if your donkey is treading grain, you can muzzle away. With an absolute rendering of the law, most Americans can turn the page and move on.

But for those who believe that it is acceptable to adapt the text to new situations or who want to extract general principles of ethics, there are all sorts of opportunities that flow along a continuum. Some might only move to include other animals that tread grain. Some go further into the realm of principle and apply the law to address broader concerns of animal welfare, humane farming, or even human labor laws.

Again, for most people it is not all or nothing. Most people will grant you that faithfulness to the Ten Commandments (at least those relating to social interaction) is a good idea and good for society, even if many of the other biblical laws are cast into the fog of cultural irrelevance.

On the flip side, even those who claim absolute literal inerrancy in all matters are seldom seen stoning people, as is commanded in a number of biblical verses for a variety of crimes from adultery (Leviticus 20:10) to sassing your parents (Leviticus 20:9, Deuteronomy 21:18-21). Few are those who refuse to mix wool and linen in the same garment (Leviticus 19:19), at least on biblical grounds. We tend to mix it up in our rules as well as our garments. The trick is removing our own self-interest from the equation so that we don't end up enforcing only laws that benefit us and turning the ones we don't happen to like into more general principles.

> ## FOR **REFLECTION**
>
> **Read I Timothy 2:8 – 3:13.**
> What do you believe about this set of instructions in light of the questions about God's role in the creation of the Bible and the authority that we give the Bible in our daily lives?
>
> Do you accept all of it? None of it? Some of it?
>
> Do you see any guiding principles behind the rules?
>
> Are these rules that should apply today or are they bound to the age and place in which they were written?

Which of the boxes below comes closest to describing your own position? What do you believe about the authority of the Bible? Why? What role, if any, did God play in the creation of the Bible? Why do you think that? What questions do you still have?

	SOLE AUTHOR	INSPIRATION	HUMAN WORK
RULEBOOK	• God wrote the Bible through the direct instruction of human authors and it contains no errors of any kind • It's laws and rules are meant for all time and are to be followed to the letter	• God inspired human writers to create the Bible in their own words and from their own perspectives • It's laws and rules are meant for all time and are to be followed to the letter	• God played no role in the creation of the Bible • Human authors included their own thoughts, biases and errors • It's laws and rules are meant for all time and are to be followed to the letter
PRINCIPLES	• God wrote the Bible through the direct instruction of human authors and it contains to errors of any kind • It's laws and rules are meant as general principles to guide human life	• God inspired human writers to create the Bible in their own words and from their own perspectives • It's laws and rules are meant as general principles to guide human life	• God played no role in the creation of the Bible • Human authors included their own thoughts, biases and errors • It's laws and rules are meant as general principles to guide human life
ANCIENT RELIC	• God wrote the Bible through the direct instruction of human authors and it contains to errors of any kind • It's laws and rules, however, were meant for others and have no contemporary relevance	• God inspired human writers to create the Bible in their own words and from their own perspectives • It's laws and rules, however, were meant for others and have no contemporary relevance	• God played no role in the creation of the Bible • Human authors included their own thoughts, biases and errors • It's laws and rules, however, were meant for others and have no contemporary relevance

PREPARATION FOR CHECK-IN

(Prepare for the next group session by thinking about and writing a brief response to these two questions.)

What is one thing that was new to me in this material?

What is one question that this week's topic raises for me?

HOMEWORK
(ALL STUDENTS)

☐ Read the text for Session 6.

☐ Select one of the ten archaeological topics described and search for additional information you can find out about the work being done in that area.

☐ Be prepared to share three to five additional bits of information about your selected topic at the final group session but recognize that if your group is large not everyone will have a chance to present.

EXTRA MILE
(CEU AND CERTIFICATE STUDENTS)

☐ Do the same homework assignment, but choose three topics instead of just one.

☐ Write out the additional information you have gleaned about each of the three topics but select only one for your class presentation.

ARCHAEOLOGY
AND THE BIBLE

ARCHAEOLOGY AND THE BIBLE

Even if you believe that the Bible is complete fiction, you have to admit that it is at least historical fiction. That is, it's filled with the names of actual places, people, and events during specific historical time periods. As the battle rages between those seeking to prove that every word of the Bible is factually true and those who wish to prove them wrong, the science of archaeology finds itself in the crosshairs.

We are, after all, dealing with very old writings—they're a treasure trove, and finding more of them is on every archaeologist's wish list, whether they consider them sacred or not. Indiana Jones aside, most of the archaeology projects around the world don't attract investors. Digging in the dirt looking for miniscule pieces of bone or pottery holds little interest for most people. But if there's a chance that a piece of bone was from a mastodon that slipped and fell exiting Noah's Ark, well then, you have a grant proposal—and guaranteed funding for your next dig.

Almost since the beginning of the science, archaeologists have been presented with the bane and the blessing of the Bible and those who turn to archaeology to support or refute its claims. Along the way, there have been some truly historic discoveries as well as a number of claims that only added fuel to the fire of controversy. In this chapter we'll take a look at both. Here are some archaeological puzzles—and the chance to do some sleuthing on your own.

1. WHERE IS THE GARDEN OF EDEN?

Adam and Eve in the Garden of Eden, 1543, Wolfgang Krodel d. Ä.

Although not related directly to archaeology, the war over if, when, and how God created the world is not new, nor is it likely to be resolved anytime soon. The evolution/creationism debate is beyond the scope of this study, but you need not look farther than the day's news to see one of the ways the Bible has come to prominence in the public sphere. When you go to engage your school board about what your children are being taught, being ignorant of the Bible puts you at a disadvantage.

If you take the story of Adam and Eve in the Garden of Eden as a literal event, you'll find yourself asking, "So where is this Garden?" The story doesn't say it was ruined or eliminated—Adam and Eve were simply kicked out and angels with flaming swords barred their re-entry. Well, who wouldn't want to rediscover that garden? The Bible gives some clues in Genesis 2:10–14:

> A river watering the garden flowed from Eden; from there it was separated into four headwaters.[11] The name of the first is the Pishon; it winds through the entire land of Havilah, where there is gold.[12] (The gold of that land is good; aromatic resin and onyx are also there.)[13] The name of the second river is the Gihon; it winds through the entire land of Cush.[14] The name of the third river is the Tigris; it runs along the east side of Ashur. And the fourth river is the Euphrates.

Anybody who deployed to Iraq during the Second Gulf War knows where the Tigris and Euphrates Rivers are, but debates rage about the identity and location of both the Pishon and the Gihon. There are also controversies over the English translation and whether the Hebrew really indicates that the Garden was the source of all four rivers. And, when all else fails, you can always claim that of course those other rivers can't be identified because the geography was completely altered after...

2. THE FLOOD AND NOAH'S ARK

Of all the questions archaeologists and geologists have considered in light of biblical writings, the event with the most supporting evidence is the Great Flood. Of course, the disagreements rage about exactly when that was, why it occurred, and how much area it covered. But a lot of water did appear to hit a lot of places all at once with catastrophic force sometime back in pre-history.

There are over two hundred stories from cultures in the Middle East, the Americas, India, China, and other areas that report a great flood. In about 70 percent of those narratives, someone is saved in a boat. The story closest to the Genesis account is found in the Epic of Gilgamesh, from the ancient civilization of Sumer. Gilgamesh was a Sumerian king who reigned in what is now Iraq and Kuwait in about the twenty-sixth century B.C.E. The literary epic bearing his name was found by nineteenth-century archaeologists amid the ruins of a library in Nineveh, in modern Iraq.

When stories or laws from other cultures echo biblical stories and laws, the question of origin always arises. Did stories simply pass from culture to culture or were they all original stories based in the same event or a common moral framework? When it comes to the flood, geologists chime in with the literary evidence and say, yes. There *was* a big flood. In lots of places.

What about the ark? First, remember that the ark Indiana Jones was searching for was *not* Noah's Ark. The word "ark" means a place of protection and safety, and there were two important arks in the Bible. Indiana Jones was after the Ark of the Covenant, which was supposed to house the Ten Commandments, and we'll look at that later. But that place of safety for the Ten Commandments was a box, not a boat.

Noah's place of protection and safety needed to be seaworthy, so his ark was built to protect the people and animals from the flood. The Bible reports (Genesis 8:4) that when the flood waters receded, the ark was able to land on "the mountains of Ararat." There is, in fact, a Mt. Ararat. In fact, there are two—the greater peak (elevation 16,854 ft.) and the lesser peak (elevation 12,782 ft.). They are both part of a dormant volcano on the Turkish/Iranian border.

Excavation site for Noah's Ark, near Mount Ararat in Turkey

Despite the enormous political difficulties (not to mention the difficulties of excavating on a high mountain), many teams of various persuasions have tried to find the ark. Paul Zimansky, an archaeologist from the State University of New York at Stony Brook, put it aptly: "I don't know of any expedition that ever went looking for the ark that didn't find it."[3] The History Channel did a special on the searches back in 2001 and had no shortage of material. But there's no consensus that it has been found—and no evidence to prove or disprove the popular myth that the unicorns were denied access to it.

The Bible doesn't mention on which of the two peaks Noah landed, but logic dictates that if it were the first bit of land to be uncovered, it would be the taller of the two. However, logic also dictates that if you've landed on the only bit of unflooded land on the earth at an elevation of almost seventeen thousand feet, you're going to need some wood for a fire, utensils, perhaps some pens for the livestock further down the slope. And there's this boat you don't need anymore…

3. WERE THERE HEBREW SLAVES IN EGYPT?

Perhaps the most pivotal narrative of the entire Old Testament is the story of Moses and the Exodus. The book of Exodus is devoted to this event and the book of Deuteronomy tells much of it again from a slightly different perspective. As the book of Genesis ends, Joseph, one of Jacob's twelve sons, is sold as a slave to an Egyptian

Khafre Pyramid at Giza

caravan and manages to use his wits and gifts in dream interpretation to gain power in Egypt, becoming second in command to Pharaoh himself.

The Genesis story goes on to tell of the rest of Jacob's family—about seventy in all—being driven to Egypt during a famine (which Joseph had managed to plan for in Egypt) and settling there to live as shepherds. By the time the next book—Exodus—opens, generations have gone by and those descendants of Jacob's family have so grown in numbers over time that the new Pharaoh–too

---

3 Ker Than, "Noah's Ark Found in Turkey?" National Geographic Daily News (April 28, 2010).

far removed from Joseph's time to remember him—is afraid. In an act of sheer political fear-mongering and manipulation, Pharaoh addresses the Egyptians in Exodus 1:9–10:

> "Look," he said to his people, "the Israelites have become far too numerous for us.[10] Come, we must deal shrewdly with them or they will become even more numerous and, if war breaks out, will join our enemies, fight against us and leave the country."

Next thing you know, the people who came to Egypt as honored guests are enslaved and are put to work building cities for Pharaoh. They do that for some four hundred years before Moses comes along to lead them out of slavery and into the Promised Land.

A lot of archaeology has been done in Egypt and we know a good bit about its history, its magnificent monuments, and its kings. So the question arises: Is any of this story of slavery documented outside the Bible? There were certainly slaves in Egypt, but were there foreign slaves who managed to escape en masse? Who was the Pharaoh of the Exodus? The Bible mentions no name.

It's a complicated set of questions. For a college graduation gift I was given a week at the Chautauqua Institution in Chautauqua, New York, to attend a seminar sponsored by *Biblical Archaeology Review* magazine. We spent the entire time listening to arguments about whether the Exodus time frame was closer to 1500 B.C.E. or 1200 B.C.E. Of course we should always bear in mind that there are those who see the Exodus story as a literary creation, or as a sacred story with only symbolic truth, with no anchor in history at all. But for those who believe that the Exodus narrative has at least some basis in history, the arguments cluster around those two time periods.

If you choose to do further research on this question, start by looking up the Hyksos. The Egyptian name means "foreign rulers"; in Arabic it means "shepherd kings." The Hyksos first appear in the literature of the eleventh dynasty; they ruled lower Egypt by the fifteenth dynasty and were expelled in the seventeenth. Equating the Hyksos with the Hebrews would argue (among other things) for the earlier date. That would make the Pharaoh of the Exodus either Amenhotep II or Thutmose III.

But the Bible also mentions that the slaves were put to work on enormous building projects and the great builder of Egypt was Ramses II (or Ramses the Great), who ruled Egypt for a full sixty-seven years during the thirteenth century B.C.E. He was the third pharaoh of the nineteenth dynasty, and he erected more cities, temples, and monuments than any other pharaoh. The pyramids, however, predate Ramses II by about fifteen hundred years. Hollywood opted for Ramses II, brilliantly played by Yul Brynner in the 1956 film *The Ten Commandments*, but the matter is by no means settled and probably never will be.

4. MT. SINAI, THE TEN COMMANDMENTS, AND THE ARK OF THE COVENANT

Still within the biblical story of the Exodus is the forty-year period when the freed Hebrew slaves wander in the desert wilderness between Egypt and Palestine, the region now known as the Sinai Peninsula. The central event of this part of the story is the group's arrival at Mt. Sinai, lots of thunder and lightning, and Moses climbing the mountain to receive the stone tablets containing the Ten Commandments.

By now it should come as no surprise that there are several mountains in the area that could qualify as Mt. Sinai, and where people can disagree, they will. The Bible doesn't mention anything being left behind on the mountain (except for the fragments from the first set of tablets that Moses smashes in rage when he sees the people worshiping a golden calf) so this controversy won't be resolved by digging for artifacts. Some passages in the Bible refer to Mt. Sinai, others to Mt. Horeb. It's generally, but not universally, assumed that these two names refer to the same mountain.

One might assume that Mt. Sinai would lie within the Sinai Peninsula, but the peninsula took its name from one of the assumed locations, not the other way around. It wasn't called the Sinai Peninsula until sometime after the first century C.E. The first-century historian Josephus claims the mountain lay somewhere in the Roman province that comprised modern Jordan, southern modern Syria, the Sinai Peninsula, and northwestern Saudi Arabia. Paul's letters simply put it in "Arabia." That's a wide area and gives you lots of mountains to choose from, with five or six having their proponents.

But wherever that mountain was, Moses climbed it and, according to both Exodus and Deuteronomy, received tablets of stone with God's law inscribed on them. Again, you don't have to look far in American culture to see the relevance this story has for contemporary politics. Everybody, it seems, wants to put reproductions of those stone tablets up or take them down in courthouses, village squares, or public schools.

What God actually had Moses do with them, however, wasn't to put them on display but to put them in a box, along with a couple of other items from the Exodus story. That box was an ark—a place of safety and protection, just like Noah's Ark had been in the storm. This place of safety, however, had to be portable, since it was to travel with a nomadic people. So it had some poles attached and priests assigned to carry it. With the law of God inside, it also doubled as a judge's bench, and Moses sat on it as he heard the cases of the people. The Ten Commandments were the covenant, or agreement, between God and the Israelites, so the ark that contained them became known as the Ark of the Covenant.

Stories of the Ark of the Covenant appear with frequency from that point forward and the ark becomes known as an object of great power, granting victory to the Israelites when they have it with them, bringing blessing to Israelite towns and cities that house it and great curses and destruction to opposing forces that dare to capture it. There is even an account of one poor soul named Uzzah who reaches out to steady the ark when its carriers stumble and gets zapped with lightning for his trouble (2 Samuel 6:6).

Artistic reconstruction of the Ark of the Covenant

Eventually the ark comes to sit in the Temple in Jerusalem, but then it disappears. Was it taken or destroyed when Jerusalem was sacked and the Temple leveled in the sixth century B.C.E.? Did someone realize that danger and hide it in a place we've yet to find? Is it still somewhere below the Temple Mount? Does it still have the Ten Commandments in it? Did it ever? Again, the question is fun enough that not only Hollywood, but also the History Channel, have explored it. A group of Ethiopian Christians claim to have it in a little town called Aksum. Trouble is, even the head of the Ethiopian church is not allowed to see it. The alleged ark is guarded by virgin monks who are, once anointed, never allowed to leave the chapel grounds except to be taken to their final resting place.

One of the challenges in trying to answer this question is the frustration of archaeologists who would like to excavate (for a myriad of reasons) below...

5. THE TEMPLE MOUNT IN JERUSALEM

When the Israelites finally make their way out of the desert, they gradually change from a tribal structure, loosely ruled by a variety of charismatic leaders called judges (a book of the Bible with that name tells that story), and decide it's time for a king (1 Samuel 8:6). The Bible records that God didn't think that was such a good idea, and in fact took it rather personally, telling Samuel (1 Samuel 8:7–9):

South wall at Temple Mount in Jerusalem

> Listen to the voice of the people in all that they say to you; for they have not rejected you, but they have rejected me from being king over them.⁸ Just as they have done to me, from the day I brought them up out of Egypt to this day, forsaking me and serving other gods, so also they are doing to you.⁹ Now then, listen to their voice; only—you shall solemnly warn them, and show them the ways of the king who shall reign over them.

The people get their way, and get their king. Eventually the kings settle in Jerusalem and the Ark of the Covenant settles there, too. With no need to move it around anymore, the third king, Solomon, comes along and builds a permanent Temple in Jerusalem to house the ark and to provide the center of worship for Israel.

But the Temple wasn't built in any old place. It was built on an already sacred site in Jerusalem, the mountain of Moriah, where Abraham offered his son Isaac to God as a sacrifice, an offering God stops at the very last minute. You can read the story in Genesis 22. But—surprise, surprise—there's no agreement that the Temple Mount is, in fact, Mt. Moriah.

Part of the issue is that Moriah was known as a mountain *range* as well as an individual mountain. And the question is further complicated by one camp that believes the Temple Mount to be Mt. Zion, the location of an old fortress that King David conquered and where he built his palace. Most scholars believe this ancient location is on a mountain near Jerusalem but is not the site of today's Temple Mount in Jerusalem. (1 Samuel 5 and 1 Chronicles 11).

In either case, the Temple built by Solomon, rebuilt by Ezra and Nehemiah in 516 B.C.E. after its destruction by the Babylonians, and enlarged by King Herod during the time of Jesus, was on holy ground already. Putting the Temple there sealed the site as the place where Israel knew God would dwell forever.

The Temple Mount is the holiest site in Judaism and is, of course, sacred to Christians as well, due to Jesus' associations with it and the Jewish roots of Christianity. The Temple Mount is also the third holiest site for Sunni Islam and is believed to be the site of Mohammad's ascension into heaven.

So it's no wonder the Temple Mount is a place that archaeologists would love to excavate for all sorts of reasons—but doing so is almost impossible because of the warring religious and political factions that continue to make it a point of struggle.

Yet some excavations have been done: Tunnels, walls, and other items have been found, though the discovery of the ark has still eluded archaeologists. Students who choose to research this topic need only search on "Temple Mount excavations" to find as much material as they'd care to discover—and more.

6. THE WALLS OF JERICHO

Taking a step backward in time, it would be unforgivable to talk of archaeology in Palestine without mentioning the work of Dame Kathleen Kenyon and her excavations in Jericho.

The book of Deuteronomy, the last book in the Pentateuch, ends with the death of Moses and the appointment of Joshua to move the Israelites out of the desert wilderness and into the land "flowing with milk and honey," known to them as the Promised Land. This is where Abraham and his descendants had lived before the famine, and the Israelites had brought the bones of Joseph all the way back with them from Egypt to bury with his ancestors.

Problem was, it had been many centuries since Abraham, Isaac, and Jacob—and a number of other peoples were now living in the land. There had been others there when Abraham had first come as well, but he had managed to work out a relationship with them and, aside from a few disputes over wells, they lived peaceably together.

But times had changed, cities had been built, and the peoples living in the Promised Land—also known as Canaan—had no intention of making room for the thousands of Israelites at their doorstep. For their part, the Israelites had no intention of asking for permission. Believing that God had promised them the land and vowing to brook no alliances with pagan nations, Joshua marched his people in for what becomes known as the Conquest.

Ruins of the Walls of Jericho

This series of battles is recorded in the book of Joshua and archaeologists have been trying to find the cities mentioned in it and document their destruction by Joshua. In general, the findings have indicated that there was a period of conquest, but that it took place over a much longer period of time than the book of Joshua leads us to think and that there were more peaceable takeovers and alliances than the Israelites claimed they made.

The most famous conquest story in the book of Joshua is the sacking of the city of Jericho, and many are the Sunday School children who have sung the African American spiritual "Joshua fit the battle of Jericho" ("…and the walls came a' tumblin' down.") The story begins in Joshua 5:13–6:27 and is one of those must-read stories of the Bible. Archaeologist Dame Kathleen Kenyon was one of millions of people who have been fascinated with the story.

Born in 1906, Kenyon was the daughter of Sir Frederic Kenyon, a biblical scholar and the director of the British Museum. She became an archaeologist of Neolithic culture in the Fertile Crescent, the swath of land in the Middle East that stretches in an arc from the Nile to the Tigris and Euphrates, covering modern-day Israel, Lebanon, Jordan, Syria, and Iraq and extending from the Mediterranean to the Persian Gulf. Kenyon led some significant excavations at the Temple Mount as well as many other places. The accomplishments that earned her world fame, however, were her excavations at Jericho from 1952 to1958. She was neither the first nor the last to excavate there, but her findings are the most significant as well as the most debated.

Jericho is currently within the Palestinian territories of the West Bank and excavations have uncovered settlements as early as 9000 B.C.E., making it the one of the oldest continuously inhabited cities in the world. Kenyon did indeed find a complete destruction of the walls of Jericho, but her findings indicated that they were destroyed well before the time Joshua would have arrived. Her findings seemed to call the veracity of the entire Old Testament into question.

Her dating methods, however, based on broken pottery fragments, have been questioned in subsequent work. Did Joshua fight the battle of Jericho? Look at the evidence and see what you think.

7. THE DEAD SEA SCROLLS

The year was 1947; the place, Israel. A young Bedouin shepherd boy was trying hard to get his sheep headed in the same direction. That's not an easy task, especially for a boy on his own. He did what he could—he threw a rock and then heard a crash. He knew that sheep don't making crashing sounds when rocks hit them, so he went to investigate. His rock had gone into a cave, smashed a ceramic pot, and out spilled the mother lode of archaeological discoveries.

Donald W. Parry, BYU, studying The Great Isaiah Scroll

In the pot (and in others like it across eleven caves near the Dead Sea) were scrolls—972 of them. They were two-thousand-year-old copies of the Bible, making up about 40 percent of the cache, plus a variety of other writings. Remember that we have never found any "originals" of the biblical writings, but prior to 1947, the earliest copies we had were from about a millennium after the birth of Christ. This finding gave us copies of biblical texts a thousand years older than any we previously had. The discovery unearthed (or rather un-potted) at least a fragment from every book in the Hebrew Bible except Esther. The most ink was devoted to the book of Psalms (thirty-nine manuscripts) and the least to 1 and 2 Samuel (four manuscripts).

Who wrote these manuscripts and why were they stashed in jars and hidden in caves? Good question—and if you think scholars agree on the answer, then you don't know scholars very well. The most widely held theory is that they were the scrolls of a Jewish sect called the Essenes, who lived a monastic life waiting for the Messiah in the community now known as Qumran. It's even been suggested that John the Baptist might have been raised in this ascetic desert community.

The Romans, sometime between C.E. 66 and C.E. 72, destroyed the group when the Jews rose up in revolt over Roman oppression and lost. Many think the Essenes saw this coming and thus hid their precious scrolls in jars throughout area caves. It's a similar theory to those on what the priests in the Jerusalem Temple might have done with the Ark of the Covenant—the Temple, after all, was destroyed during this uprising as well.

Due to political haggling, it took decades for scholars to get their hands on these scrolls to begin their work, and their riches have still not been exhausted. One notable finding, however, was the discovery of just how careful Jewish scribes were in copying their Scriptures. It's easy to think that when you're dealing with copies of copies of copies that you'll end up with something like the child's game of "gossip," where what's whispered to the last person bears little to no resemblance to what the first person said. But that proved not to be the case.

Even though the copies were a thousand years older than the copies we had, it was obvious that every copier, at least from that point forward, had been meticulous and careful. Which is not to say there weren't any differences. But perhaps those we already had were copies of different, older versions? We can't say. But we can say that this is the most significant archaeological find of the Christian Era.

8. THE LIFE OF JESUS

Was Jesus a historical figure? The consensus of scholars of all types and all faiths—and even atheist critics who think the Gospels are complete myths—is that the odds are strongly in favor of a man named Jesus who lived in first-century Palestine and was executed by the Romans for sedition. That belief is not universal, and there have been those across time who have argued against his existence as a historical personage.

The James ossuary was on display at the Royal Ontario Museum from November 15, 2002 to January 5, 2003

The doubters are in the minority, but ultimately it's not something that can be proved by scientific or historical methods. There are a number of sources outside the Bible that reference Jesus—it's been said that there is more historical evidence for the existence of Jesus than for the existence of Napoleon—but neither side can prove their point beyond any doubt. I understand the difficulty. When I was doing genealogy work on my family, I had a hard time proving the existence of my grandfather. So affirming that someone existed two thousand years ago is a very tall order.

In 2002, the Biblical Archaeology Society announced a significant find. In the hands of an Israeli antiquities collector and engineer named Oded Golan was a two-thousand-year-old ossuary—a chalk box of the kind used to hold the bones of the dead. Inscribed in Aramaic on the side were the words "James, son of Joseph, brother of Jesus." If genuine, it could be the oldest possible evidence of the existence of Jesus, although all three names (James, Joseph, and Jesus) were common ones and this ossuary could have belonged to a different family unit.

The age of the box has been confirmed, but the Israeli Antiquities Authority claimed that the inscription is a later forgery. In 2004, Oded Golan was charged with forty-four counts of forgery, fraud, and deception. The case was tried in October 2010, but as of April 2011 no verdict had been reached. One more fun thing for scholars to debate.

When it comes to evidence for the life and deeds of Jesus, there isn't much archaeology can say about the matter. If you've ever taken a religious tour of Israel, you'll know that for every site that purports to be a place where Jesus did something, there seem to be six others competing for the very same honor. That is even true of the places of Jesus' birth, death, and resurrection, let alone other, lesser events in his life. When I visited in 2007, guides showed me the site where Jesus supposedly ascended into heaven, and they claimed that an indentation in a rock was his actual footprint. I may just be overly skeptical, but I don't recall in the biblical account of the ascension that anyone looked down and exclaimed, "OMG! His footprint is right there in the rock!"

Tour guides even showed me the location of the inn where the Good Samaritan took the man found by the side of the road—a neat trick, since that story is a parable. Fiction. A story Jesus made up to make a point. The guides may have been correct that these were the ruins of an inn, and maybe a wounded traveler or two had stopped there. Maybe Jesus even imagined that particular inn as he told the story. But it was most definitely not the location of a fictional event.

The cities Jesus traveled to can be identified and visited, but it's often hard to get a sense of what it would have been like in the first century because traditional sites usually got marked by one or more shrines, churches, or monasteries. But archaeology can't prove what happened in those places, only that they existed, whether or not they were destroyed at some point, and how the people in those places lived.

It's the same with all the little splinters that claim to be a piece of the "true cross." Archaeologists can date the wood and tell you whether or not it came from the right time period. Maybe there's some way to tell that it once was part of a cross—that brutal means of execution was commonplace and there were many crosses in that time. There were at least three on that very day and in the same location where Jesus died. But there is no way to either prove or disprove that a certain piece of wood was part of the cross on which Jesus died. That is something that must be taken (or not) on faith.

9. THE SHROUD OF TURIN

The greatest archaeological puzzle of them all is the Shroud of Turin, the piece of cloth that many believe to be the shroud covering the crucified Jesus, the image of his traumatized face and body captured in the cloth in a photographic negative. The wounds and trauma to the body coincide with the description of Jesus' passion as found in the Gospels.

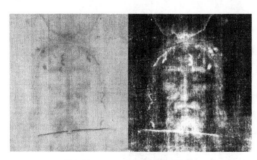
Head image on the Shroud of Turin

Even if the shroud is a forgery, it's an old and mysterious one. It first turned up in the Middle Ages and the image was quite faint. It wasn't until Italian photographer Secondo Pia took the very first photograph of the shroud on May 28, 1898 that observers noticed that the image was much more clearly defined in the photographic negative. In fact, the negative image was actually the positive and the fainter image on the cloth the negative.

In 1988, some of the cloth was taken for radiocarbon testing, which showed that the sample dated to between 1260 and 1390 C.E. However, some argue that since the cloth that was cut to be sampled was (naturally) not a part that contained the image, some sections of the cloth could be older.

The truly fascinating piece, however, is that those who have examined the shroud for signs of forgery have found none and no one has yet to replicate the image using any technique available in the Middle Ages. In fact, modern technology cannot determine how the image got there at all, let alone how it got there with medieval or earlier technology.

The Roman Catholic Church has neither verified nor disputed the claim that it is the burial shroud of Jesus, and it rests today in the Cathedral of St. John the Baptist in Turin, Italy. From time to time it is placed on public display.

10. OTHER FINDS RELATED TO THE NEW TESTAMENT

With the exception of finding new stores of previously unknown texts (the Bible mentions a letter Paul wrote to the Laodiceans that has never been found), the most helpful thing archaeology can do for the New Testament is to help us understand what life in first-century Palestine was like. In the town of Capernaum you can see the foundations of a home where some believe Peter

The "Jesus Boat" on display in Tiberias, Israel

might have lived. It was found in 1906 but not really excavated until 1968 to 1998. No proof, of course, since Peter neglected to carve "Peter lived here" in the rock, but the site reveals a first-century house in Peter's hometown that was evidently used as an early Christian gathering place. That tells us a lot about how Peter and others in that area lived, whether it was truly his home or not.

The same is true of the more recent find of a first-century fishing boat in the mud under the Sea of Galilee. Discovered in the 1980s, it quickly became known as the "Jesus boat." There's no way to tell if Jesus ever set foot in that particular boat, but the finding shows us what the boats Jesus and his disciples used on the Sea of Galilee might have looked like, and helps us enter the stories in the Gospels in new ways.

Archaeologists have found an inscription bearing the name of Pontius Pilate and an ossuary containing the bones of the high priest Caiaphas, both of which point to the fact that whatever else you think of the stories told in the New Testament, they were based in particular historical time-frames and locations with leading figures that have evidence outside the Bible for their existence and influence.

SCIENCE AND FAITH

It's generally a mistake to look to the science of archaeology (or any other science, for that matter) to prove or disprove biblical accounts. Such expectations taint the spirit of objectivity on which all science rests. Science cannot prove or disprove matters of faith and faith cannot prove or disprove matters of scientific inquiry. They are separate and distinct ways of discovering and defining "truth."

When science and faith are each given their proper role, however, the glorious canvas of life on earth across the millennia begins to take shape with all its nuance, beauty, and mystery. If you're determined to find yellow, you will see only yellow. But if you let the canvas speak for itself, you'll discover gold and mustard and saffron, cream and apricot and lemon. It might be difficult to say if a part is gold or brown, amber or orange—but those questions then simply become the starting point for your next adventure.

CONCLUSION

Sort of. When you're dealing with Bible study there's no such thing as a conclusion. If this study has been successful, you now have more (although perhaps different) questions than you did when you started. Learning to love questions more than answers is the key to exciting and rewarding Bible study. Each question leads to new doors of discovery of all kinds, and an entire lifetime is not enough to open and explore them all.

With this study you've merely scratched the surface. Subsequent studies in this series will take you deeper, provide answers to some of the questions you have now, and give you a whole new set of questions to work from. Ideally your questions become not just questions of content and information, but questions of human nature, spiritual life, and living together in community—the large questions that can't be delegated to computers but that life will ask of us at some point along the way. You may or may not find that the Bible provides answers to those questions, but the Bible can certainly provide a springboard for asking them.

PREPARATION FOR CHECK-IN

(Prepare for the last group session by thinking about and writing a brief response to these two questions.)

What is one thing that was new to me in this material?

What is one question that this week's topic raises for me?

HOMEWORK

- ☐ *If you are not at the final class session or if you have not been part of a group*, fill out the evaluation in Appendix 1 of this text and return it to the Massachusetts Bible Society, 199 Herrick Rd., Newton Center, MA 02459 or via e-mail to admin@massbible.org. (A copy can be found in the first appendix of this text.)

EXTRA MILE

(CEU AND CERTIFICATE STUDENTS)

- ☐ Prepare a final essay of five hundred to seven hundred words describing your experience with the course and its contents. Have your views of the Bible changed? If so, in what way(s)? Were your views of the Bible confirmed? In what way(s)? What unanswered questions about the Bible are most important to you now?

- ☐ Submit this essay to your facilitator or to the Massachusetts Bible Society along with any other outstanding materials needed for your certification.

WHAT NOW?

THERE'S MORE I WANT TO KNOW!

If you have reached this point and feel like this course has not provided nearly enough information, then I have done my job. Yes, this course barely scratches the surface, but it is my hope that it scratched the surface enough to have you at least a bit more intrigued about what might lie underneath.

It appears to be one of the hallmarks of education that the more we learn, the less we know—in other words, our education shows us just how vast and complex any field truly is compared to what we can say we "know" about it. I know it feels counterintuitive, but if the course has been successful, you will come out feeling like you know less than you did at the start. When I graduated from seminary, the name of my new "Master of Divinity" degree made me laugh out loud. Master? I think not. We're talking big subjects here.

My advice to you? Keep digging…just like those archaeologists you read about. Keep exploring the territory; there are treasures in the field.

As you may remember from the Introduction, there are four, six-week courses that comprise *The Dickinson Series: Exploring the Bible*. This is just the first of those four courses and serves as a broad overview of topics that will be explored in more depth in the other three. You can find descriptions of all four courses on page iv of this text.

Of course there are literally thousands of resources for Bible study out there in addition to formal programs of study in colleges and seminaries. If you are part of a church community there are probably Bible studies going on all around you. If there aren't, you may have to pull out the jumper cables and get things started. You can find other curriculum resources on our website at **massbible.org/mass-bible-curricula**.

But if you like the way we do things in the Dickinson Series, then I invite you to take the next course or two or three and to…

JOIN THE DICKINSON SERIES COMMUNITY

The world of the Bible is a world of community—a focus that often flies under the radar in the individualism of the contemporary Western world. If you have taken this course as part of a small group, you will have seen the benefits (and perhaps some of the pitfalls!) of joining with others to reach a common goal. It is in community where we can test our theories, explore our questions, and find our way when our own GPS can't find the satellite.

Whether or not you take other courses, we at the Massachusetts Bible Society want to help you get and stay connected to a community of people who share your desire to explore the Bible. You can do that in several ways.

The most immediate way to stay connected is to join and engage the Dickinson Series Community Forums at **biblit.massbible.org**. You can post thoughts, questions, or other issues for discussion and feedback at any time and from any place. It's free and nobody will bug you to buy things (except for when a spammer sneaks through the spam controls!).

You can also gather with people at our annual Dickinson Series Conference, held each May/June (see p. iv). Hear some great lectures, attend workshops, explore resources, and engage in fellowship with others who have some of the same questions that you do. If you're enrolled in the Certificate in Biblical Literacy program, this is where you will graduate.

You might also consider joining the Dickinson Series Alumni. Your dues will entitle you to a variety of discounts and helps to provide scholarship assistance for those without means who would like to take Dickinson Series courses. You can find out more and join at **massbible.org/dickinson-series-alumni**.

At the very least we hope you'll allow us to keep in touch via e-mail and will pass along items of interest to your friends. "Like" us on Facebook, and be sure to keep in touch. We want to know where your exploring takes you!

APPENDIX I

STUDENT EVALUATION FOR *WHAT IS THE BIBLE?*

Why did you take this course? Were your expectations met?

Did you do this study with a group or on your own? (*If you did it on your own please skip to the last question on p. 90.*)

Did you take this course for certification or CEUs?   Yes   No

(*If yes, please be sure that all of your written work is submitted to the Massachusetts Bible Society by either yourself or your group facilitator at the conclusion of the course.*)

Did your group have a mix of "Extra Mile" and informal students? Yes No

    If "yes," did you find the mix helpful? Yes No

    Why or why not?

```



```

Who was your group facilitator? _____

Please rate your facilitator from 1–10 on the following items with 1 being the least positive and 10 being the most positive.

    Creating a welcoming and inclusive environment _____

    Keeping the class sessions on track _____

    Beginning and ending on time _____

    Handling conflicting opinions with respect _____

    Being prepared for class sessions _____

Please rate the following aspects of the physical setting for your group with 1 being "poor" and 10 being "excellent."

    The space was free of distractions and interruptions _____

    The environment was physically comfortable and conducive to learning _____

    The group could easily adjust to different configurations _____

    It was easy to see instructional materials and group members _____

    Restroom facilities were easily accessible _____

    The space was accessible to those with disabilities _____

Do you have a particular faith tradition or spiritual orientation? If so, how would you name it?

```



```

Did you feel that your opinions and perspective were respected in the course materials? Yes   No

        In the class discussions? Yes   No   N/A

        By the facilitator? Yes   No   N/A

If you were an "informal student" (i.e. not a student seeking certification or CEUs), how much of the homework and reading did you complete? Please describe on a scale of 1–10, with 1 being virtually none of it and 10 being all of it. _____

Did you do any of the Extra Mile assignments? Yes   No

Please rate the quality of the homework assignments on a scale of 1–10 (with 1 being the most negative and 10 being the most positive) on the following:

        It was easy to understand the assignment _____

    The work could reasonably be completed between sessions _____

      I learned important things from doing the homework _____

      I did not feel pushed to come to a particular conclusion _____

Did you visit the online forums for the Dickinson Series? To what degree did you engage with others on these forums?

Did this study answer any questions you had at the beginning? What were some of the most important questions that were answered for you?

Did anything disappoint you in this study? Was there something you expected that was not provided? Questions you really wanted answered that were not?

What new questions do you have upon completion that you did not have at the beginning? Do you find those new questions exciting or frustrating?

Did you learn anything of interest to you from this study? If you studied with a group, indicate how much of that came from the material provided and how much from the group discussion.

Have your impressions/beliefs/thoughts about the Bible changed as a result of this study? In what way?

Would you recommend this study to a friend?

On a scale of 1–10 with 1 being not at all helpful and 10 being exceptionally helpful, how would you rate this study? _____

Other thoughts, comments or suggestions:

Please return this evaluation to:
Massachusetts Bible Society, 199 Herrick Rd.,
Newton Center, MA 02459
or e-mail to admin@massbible.org.

APPENDIX 2

MASSACHUSETTS BIBLE SOCIETY STATEMENT ON SCRIPTURE

The Massachusetts Bible Society is an ecumenical, Christian organization with a broad diversity of Scriptural approaches and interpretations among its members and supporters. The following statement on the nature of Scripture represents the guiding principle for our selection of programming and resources, but agreement with it is neither a prerequisite for membership nor a litmus test for grant recipients.

> The Bible was written by many authors, all inspired by God. It is neither a simple collection of books written by human authors, nor is it the literal words of God dictated to human scribes. It is a source of religious truth, presented in a diversity of styles, genres, and languages and is not meant to serve as fact in science, history, or social structure.

> The Bible has authority for communities of faith who take time to study and prayerfully interpret its message, but it is also important for anyone who wants more fully to understand culture, religious thought, and the world in which we live.

> Biblical texts have been interpreted in diverse ways from generation to generation and are always filtered through the lens of the reader's faith and life experiences. This breadth and plurality, however, are what keep the Bible alive through the ages and enhance its ongoing, transformative power.

APPENDIX 3

A COVENANT FOR BIBLE STUDY

We covenant together to deal with our differences in a spirit of mutual respect and to refrain from actions that may harm the emotional and physical well-being of others.

The following principles will guide our actions:

- We will treat others whose views may differ from our own with the same courtesy we would want to receive ourselves.

- We will listen with a sincere desire to understand the point of view being expressed by another person, especially if it is different from our own.

- We will respect each other's ideas, feelings, and experiences.

- We will refrain from blaming or judging in our attitude and behavior towards others.

- We will communicate directly with any person with whom we may disagree in a respectful and constructive way.

- We will seek feedback to ensure that we have truly understood each other in our communications.

APPENDIX 4

HELP! I HAVE QUESTIONS!

- If the question is specific to a particular Bible passage, look in the notes associated with that passage in your study Bible. Are there notes that address the question? Does someone else in your group have a different study Bible? Does it have any helpful notes?

- Google is your friend. It is quite likely that if you type your question into an Internet search engine verbatim, you will come up with more "answers" than you thought possible. Ditto for just putting in a Bible verse reference. These results, however, are unfiltered and will range from well-informed responses to the conclusions of the truly unbalanced or the simply ignorant. It is sometimes difficult to tell the difference if you don't have a biblical education yourself, so approach this option with caution. It will, however, give you a sense of the range of ideas out there.

- Submit the question to the Ask-a-Prof service of the Massachusetts Bible Society. This is a free service that takes your question to thirty-five professors from seminaries and universities across the US and the UK. Participating professors come from a variety of denominations and faith traditions and represent both liberal and conservative viewpoints. You can read more about them and ask your question at massbible.org/ask-a-prof.

- Register and use the Dickinson Series Community forums on our website to discuss your questions with students in other groups and the Massachusetts Bible Society staff. You can find them at biblit.massbible.org.

- Ask your facilitator or a religious leader you trust for help.

- Remember that not all questions have "answers" per se. Sometimes a variety of opinions will be the best you can do.

ABCDEFGHIJKLMNOPQRSTUVWXYZ

APPENDIX 5

GLOSSARY

A.D.
Abbreviation for the Latin *Anno Domini*, meaning "in the year of the Lord." A system of notating time, generally used with B.C.

Antichrist
With a small "a" it is one who denies or opposes Christ. With a capital "A" it refers to a great antagonist expected to fill the world with wickedness but to be conquered forever by Christ at his second coming. Mentioned in the Bible in the book of Revelation.

Apocrypha
Books included in the Septuagint and Vulgate but excluded from the Jewish and Protestant canons of the Old Testament.

Apocalypse
One of the Jewish and Christian writings of 200 B.C.E. to 150 C.E. marked by pseudonymity, symbolic imagery, and the expectation of an imminent cosmic cataclysm in which God destroys the ruling powers of evil and raises the righteous to life in a messianic kingdom.

Ark
Something that affords protection and safety. Two different forms of this are prominent in the Bible. One is a boat—Noah's Ark—and the other is a sacred box—the Ark of the Covenant.

Babylonian Captivity (or Exile)
The period in Jewish history during which the Jews of the ancient Kingdom of Judah were captives in Babylon—conventionally 587–538 B.C.E.

B.C.
Abbreviation for "Before Christ." A system of notating time, generally used with A.D.

B.C.E.
Abbreviation for "Before the Christian Era" or "Before the Common Era." An academic and faith-neutral notation of time. Generally used with C.E.

Canon
An authoritative list of books accepted as Holy Scripture. The word is from the Latin meaning "rule" or "standard."

Catholic
With a small "c," the word means "universal." It is used this way in the Apostles' Creed. With a capital "C" the word denotes the Roman Catholic Church.

C.E.
Abbreviation for "Christian Era" or "Common Era." An academic and faith-neutral notation of time. Generally used with B.C.E.

Codex
A manuscript book especially of Scripture, classics, or ancient annals.

Codex Sinaiticus
A fourth-century, hand-written copy of the Greek Bible.

Concordance
An alphabetical index of all the words in a text or corpus of texts, showing every contextual occurrence of a word.

Conquest
The period of Jewish history described in the biblical book of Joshua.

Covenant
A formal, solemn, and binding agreement.

Creationism
The doctrine or theory holding that matter, the various forms of life, and the world were created by God out of nothing in a way determined by a literal reading of Genesis.

Deuterocanonical
Of, relating to, or constituting the books of Scripture contained in the Septuagint but not in the Hebrew canon. Primarily Roman Catholic and Orthodox usage for the texts known to Jews and Protestants as the Apocrypha.

Dispensationalism
A system of Christian belief, formalized in the nineteenth century, that divides human history into seven distinct ages or dispensations. See the boxed description on page 61.

Evangelical
When used with a capital "E," this refers to those in Christian traditions that emphasize a high view of biblical authority, the need for personal relationship with God achieved through a conversion experience (being "born again"), and an emphasis on sharing the gospel that Jesus' death and resurrection saves us from our sins. The tradition generally deemphasizes ritual and prioritizes personal experience.

Gilgamesh
A legendary Sumerian king and hero of the *Gilgamesh Epic*, which contains a story of a great flood during which a man is saved in a boat.

**Hapax Legomenon
(pl. Hapax Legomena)**
A word or form of speech occurring only
once in a document or body of work.

Hyksos
Of or relating to a Semitic dynasty that
ruled Egypt from about the eighteenth to
the sixteenth centuries B.C.E.

Inerrancy
Exemption from error. Infallibility.

Jerome
(ca. 347 C.E.–30 September 420 C.E.) A Roman
Christian priest, confessor, theologian and
historian, and who became a Doctor of the
Church. Best known for his translation of the
Bible into Latin (the Vulgate). Recognized by
the Roman Catholic and Eastern Orthodox
churches as a saint.

LXX
See *Septuagint*

Mainline
Certain Protestant churches in the United
States that comprised a majority of Americans
from the colonial era until the early twentieth
century. The group is contrasted with evangelical and fundamentalist groups. They include
Congregationalists, Episcopalians, Methodists,
northern Baptists, most Lutherans, and
most Presbyterians, as well as some smaller
denominations.

Marcion (of Sinope)
ca. 85–160 C.E. An early Christian bishop who
believed the God of the Hebrew Scriptures
to be inferior or subjugated to the God of the
New Testament and developed his own canon of
Scripture accordingly. He was excommunicated
for his belief.

Masoretes
Groups of Jewish scribes working between the
seventh and eleventh centuries C.E. They added
vowel notations to the Hebrew Scriptures.

Mordecai Nathan (Rabbi)
Philosopher rabbi of the fifteenth century
C.E. who wrote the first concordance to the
Hebrew Bible and added numbered verse
notations to the Hebrew Bible for the first time.

Ossuary
A depository, most commonly a box, for the bones (as opposed to the entire corpse) of the dead.

Orthodox
With a capital "O" referring to the Eastern Orthodox church (and its various geographic subdivisions), the Oriental Orthodox churches (and their subdivisions), and any Western Rite Orthodox congregations allied with the above.

Pentateuch
The first five books of the Bible: Genesis, Exodus, Leviticus, Numbers, and Deuteronomy.

Protestant
Used here in the broadest sense of any Christian not of a Catholic or Orthodox church.

Pseudepigrapha
In biblical studies, the Pseudepigrapha are Jewish religious works written ca. 200 B.C.E–200 C.E., which are not part of the canon of any established Jewish or Christian tradition. See page 38.

Pharisee
A member of a Jewish sect of the intertestamental period noted for strict observance of rites and ceremonies of the written law and for insistence on the validity of their own oral traditions concerning the law.

Rapture
The term "rapture" is used in at least two senses in modern traditions of Christian theology: in pre-tribulationist views, in which a group of people will be "left behind," and as a synonym for the final resurrection generally.

Robert Stephanus
Protestant book printer living in France in the sixteenth century who divided the chapters of the New Testament into the verses we have today.

Septuagint or LXX
An ancient Greek translation of the Hebrew Scriptures. Translation began in the third century B.C.E. with the Pentateuch and continued for several centuries.

Stephen Langton
Theology professor in Paris and archbishop of Canterbury in the twelfth century who first added chapter divisions to the Bible.

A B C D E F G H I J K L M N O P Q R **S T U V W X Y Z**

Supersessionism
The idea that God's covenant with Christians
supersedes and therefore displaces God's
covenant with Israel.

Synoptic Gospels
From the Greek meaning to "see alike," the
Synoptics are Matthew, Mark, and Luke.

Testament
With a capital "T" it means either of the two
main divisions of the Bible: The Old Testament
or the New Testament. With a small "t" the
word simply means a covenant or agreement
that is formalized in writing and witnessed.

Tetragrammaton
The four consonants in Exodus 3:14 (YHWH)
that represent God's name.

Vulgate
The late fourth-century Latin translation
of the Bible done by St. Jerome.

LOOKING FOR THE
PERFECT DVD PAIRING
FOR
What is the Bible?

One Book, Many Voices

MASSACHUSETTS BIBLE SOCIETY

HOW DO YOU UNDERSTAND THE BIBLE?

CAN WE TRUST WHAT IS IN THE BIBLE?

IS THERE A RIGHT OR WRONG WAY TO READ IT?

Produced by the Massachusetts Bible Society and The Walker Group, LLC,
One Book, Many Voices will let you hear directly from scholars, clergy,
and just regular folks helping you to reflect on these questions.